W9-DDJ-013

The Oklahoma Gamblin' Man

By

Gary Rex Tanner

The Oklahoma Gamblin' Man

For more information address:
TLFP, P.O. Box 1925
Escondido, CA 92033
info@garyrextanner.com or call (800) 964-1511

Published by
Two Little Frogs Publishing
P.O. Box 1925, Escondido CA 92033

Hardcover Edition 2014

ISBN 978-09892186-5-8

ISBN 0989218651

Designed by Daisy Tanner

Printed in the United States

This book is dedicated to our long lost cousin

Steven Saris

"When the Okies left Oklahoma and migrated to California they raised the average intelligence level of both states"

Will Rogers

Contents

Acknowledgments 13
Introduction 15
Prologue 17
Born On The Fourth Of July 25
The Great Cover up 35
Bull Dog / Bull Durham 43
Red Headed Stranger 49
Claremore 55
Junkyard Dogs 65
Mexican Gold 73
The World Champion Of The Mid-West 79
Miller 89
The Oklahoma Gamblin' Man 101
The Arkansas Traveler 107
Don't Take Me Back To Tulsa 115
Pretty Boy Floyd 121
Wanted In Wichita 127
Elmer Gantry Eat Your Heart Out 139
California Here I Come 151
California Pie 159
Attacked By Indians 169
Jackpot! 177
The Girl From Missouri 185
The Shipyard 197
Return To Modesto 207
The Plumbin' Shop 213
The Final Chapter 233
Epilogue 239
About the Author 249

Pictures

Oklahoma & Surrounding Area Map 21
Sterling Lafayette Tanner (circa 1916) 26
James Tanner (circa 1925) 28
Leonard & Effie Tanner (circa 1925) 30
Tanner Children (circa 1919) 34
Leonard Garth "Buster" Tanner 42
Kilmer Tanner (circa 1921) 48
Junkyard/Bunkhouse 68
Jack Burns 72
Hotel Mason in Claremore, Oklahoma 80
Vernon Miller 93
Rex Tanner's Sisters 99
Charles "Pretty Boy" Floyd 120
Rex Albert Tanner 125
Kilmer Tanner 1933 147
Morris Tanner (circa 1933) 155
California Map 158
Modesto Arch 160
Strand Theatre 165
Elmer Tanner 1912 168
Leonard Franklin Tanner (Frank-circa 1935) 176
DeLois Bowles Tanner 186
Rex & DeLois Tanner's Wedding Day 1937 188
Orval Bowles (circa 1937) 190
"Conn" & "Tex" 1943 198
Frank & Ruby Tanner (circa 1943) 206
1948 Cadillac Fleetwood Sedan
& Tanner Family Home (1945-1952) 214
Morris & Sue Tanner 216
Modesto Bee Article-Plumbing Labor Suit 219
Modesto Bee Article-Plumbing Shop Fire 220
Modesto Bee-Plumbing Shop Fire Photos 221
World Cycles Chart 244
Gary & Daisy Tanner 249

Songs

Wind Blowin' West 22
Seven Sisters 97
Wanted In Wichita 137
Fayette's Boys 148
The Oklahoma Gamblin' Man 156
Oklahoma On My Mind 166
The Girl From Missouri 194
California Pie 224
Whistle A Sweet Melody 227
When The Goin' Gets Tough 228
The Plumbin' Shop 230
The Long Migration West 246

Paintings

Cabin 24
Frank's Mule Team 32
Airedales & Hog 36
Boys & Bulldog 46
Boys & Slingshots 52
Boys Playing Football 58
Mexican Desert Walk 76
Hopping Freight Train 82
Packard Phaeton 100
Hay Truck 134
Semi-Truck 182

Acknowledgments

I could not offer this work publicly without giving credit to my loving wife Daisy whose tireless contributions on every level make mine pale in comparison. While it is true that I wrote every word in the book, it was simply a matter of organizing stories and events that had been given to me from an original source...my father. Daisy, on the other hand, painstakingly painted original illustrations, restored and arranged old photographs, edited, proofread, researched, critiqued and organized this entire book while working at a full time job and caring for elderly parents. I could not begin to express my deep awe and appreciation for her skills and commitment to this literary effort. So Thank You Daisy, I did not expect that this writing would require the involvement that it has for you, but thank God you were there or this baby would never have gotten off the ground.

Gary Rex Tanner

Thanks to David Tanner, Scott Tanner, Leatrice Tanner Wagner, Billie Sue Tanner Falling, Kay Von Boutot, Robert Peoples, Sandra LeRoy at The National Archives of Kansas City, Teresa Ybarra Phillips for junkyard photo.

Introduction

America has been a beacon of hope and a land of opportunity since its inception. During the twentieth century, America became a great country and the Americans born during the early part of that century proved to be what some now call "America's greatest generation." There are millions of contributors to and members of that elite generation; each has a story that is unique and fascinating. The times moved fast, and change was essential and uncompromising. Rex Tanner's story is of one man who started from meager beginnings, survived everything and anything life could throw at him and retained his good humor and self-confidence until his last dying breath. An inspiration and example of the American heart, Rex Tanner's life now comes alive on these pages for all to consider.

Gary Rex Tanner

Author, Singer, Composer, Poet, Publisher, Philosopher, Psychologist, Infantryman, Master Plumber

Prologue

I never intended to write this book. In fact, I had written songs about the stories herein in the early nineteen-eighties. My close friend Kin Vassy and I co-produced an album at Lion Share Recording Studios in Beverly Hills, CA, that never quite got completed and the masters were lost due to his untimely death. I did salvage a cassette of the rough mixes and was able to share them with some family members, including the principal of most of the songs, my father, Rex Albert "Pappy" Tanner. I gave him his own copy and when I saw him a couple of days later, I asked him if he'd listened to the tape and what he thought. "Jesus Christ son, a man would do well to be careful what he says around you, boy," he replied, with no hint of whether or not he cared for the music, one way or another. When he passed a dozen years later, they brought me his Lincoln Town Car, my only inheritance from his long, colorful life. There wasn't anything of any value, or of interest to me, in the glove compartment or console, but when I punched the "eject" button on his cassette stereo player, out popped the tape I had given him. Apparently it was the only music he cared to listen to when he drove in his car.

Pappy and I had a unique relationship. After World War II, my brother was a toddler, I was five or six years old and Pappy would take me with him whenever he went out alone in the evenings and on weekends. I was a natural singer and Pappy would encourage me to sing and accompany me with his whistling. He told me to "sing from the heart" and used Louis Armstrong as an example to emulate. In the course of whatever business we were attending to, we would drop in at bars and "beer joints," where Pappy was always a welcome and respected personage. Most of the men that gathered at these places for some social interplay were mid-westerners who had ridden the hard times of the Depression into California from their homes in Oklahoma, Texas and Arkansas. The native Californians called them "Okies," a derogatory term that Pappy took delight in applying to himself whenever the opportunity arose. Most of those "ol' boys" had little or no formal education and for the most part had difficulty pronouncing my given name. Gary generally came out as Jerry, Jeery, Geery and usually was ultimately changed to "Ol' Rex's Boy."

Over his lifetime Pappy related to me all the stories that follow in this book. There was no timeline or continuity to them; they were always told individually and usually as anecdotes to illustrate some lesson or point that he wanted me to understand. He wasn't someone who lived in the past and while he might have repeated some of these experiences from time to time to friends, acquaintances and other family members, most of them have never been heard in context by anyone other than me. I have made no attempt to surround his tales with anything other than the descriptions he gave me. While it was necessary to expand his dialogue somewhat, I tell them the way I remember him telling me, sometimes without regard to the accuracy of details such as the names of incidental characters, hotels, automobiles and such. Most of the characters are authentic, as are the cities and historical events that are mentioned. The personal events that he recounted retained continuity throughout his lifetime. Occasionally, he would tell a story in the presence of a family member who was around at the time it happened and never once did anyone ever imply, verbally, or physically (such as an upward glance, or a head shake), that what he was saying wasn't exactly as he was telling it. The following are the stories he told…the stories about him could not be told in a one volume book…

The Oklahoma Gamblin' Man

Kansas
Missouri
Oklahoma
Arkansas
Texas
Leavenworth
Topeka
Kansas City
St. Louis
Lyons
Wichita
Golden City
Oologah
Collinsville
Foyhil
Claremore
Pea Ridge
Hoxie
Tulsa
Muskogee
Oklahoma City
Little Rock
Dallas
Houston
Brownsville

Wind Blowin' West

Said goodbye to our kinfolks in Virginia they say
Rollin' west to Kentucky and a sun shiny day
Jacob and Frederick had fought in the wars
To free this great land from the hands of king George

Sing hallelujah sing Rock of the Ages
We always sing Nearer My God to Thee
Some went to Georgia and some to Missouri
But Glasgow Kentucky held a sweet mystery

They said when we got there we were different from most
Plowin' fields in our dress shirts and our good Sunday coats
But they treated us kindly though we didn't fit in
Fifty years later we were back in the wind

The Civil War came and the land went for taxes
So we loaded the wagon and hitched up the team
Said goodbye to the life of the gentleman farmer
Lookin' for someplace where folks could live free

Sing hallelujah sing Rock of the Ages
We always sing Nearer My God to Thee
Some wore the blue coats and some wore the gray ones
But you choke on your pride when the land's in defeat

The old folks had died and my grandpa's grandpa
Heard of a place that they called Arkansas
Where the people were friendly and the soil rich and black
Took his young wife and he never looked back

Sing Hallelujah sing Rock of the Ages
We always sing Nearer My God to Thee
It's too far to Texas I've been to Kentucky
Due west to the Ozarks and another sweet dream

When the Arkansas Traveler met my granddaddy's daddy
He told him some stories about the Indian lands
He said "there's a fortune 'cross the Arkansas River"
For a man with six sons that can work with their hands"

So he loaded up Louis and Leonard and Elmer
Grover and Fayette and all of the rest
He said "Boys we're goin' to try Oklahoma
The country is growin' and the wind's blowin' west"

Sing Hallelujah sing Rock of the Ages
We always sing Nearer My God to Thee
There's black gold in Texas blue grass in Kentucky
New land in Oklahoma and it's waitin' for me

Words & Music by Gary Rex Tanner

Songs from this book can be heard at
www.oklahomagamblinman.com

To hear songs written & performed by Gary Rex Tanner
Please visit www.garyrextanner.com

1

Born On The Fourth Of July

It was the 4th of July 1913. Effie Tanner was heavy with child. The family was preparing for a picnic with other family members near Collinsville, Oklahoma, when Effie decided it might be too much of a test of her endurance to accompany them. This new child would be her fifth, so she was confident that she would be fine while they were gone, and she could use the time alone to prepare for the event that everyone knew would soon be coming.

Her husband Leonard, she knew, would probably be drunk and belligerent by the time the day was over and she didn't mind missing the ordeal of getting him home. Leonard had gone blind as a two year old child, unexplainably regaining his sight at around ten years old. There were few doctors capable of diagnosing something as unusual as a child suddenly losing and regaining sight, especially in Pea Ridge, Arkansas, where Leonard's family lived. When Leonard's sight suddenly returned, everyone was amazed and his brother Fayette (Sterling Lafayette Tanner), who was

Sterling Lafayette Tanner (circa 1916)

two years older than Leonard and would later in life become a Pentecostal preacher of the original Holiness Movement in the early 1920's, said he had been praying day and night for his brother to see again.

Leonard's sight didn't bring the harmony that was expected, and a family problem was soon imminent. All of Leonard's siblings had attended school, at least to some degree. They could all read and write and do arithmetic. Upon regaining his sight, Leonard was enrolled in the first grade at the country school where his brothers and sisters attended. Being big for his age, he was even more conspicuous among the six and seven year olds that were his classmates.

He was ridiculed and teased mercilessly and went home after the first day and refused to return. Nothing anyone could say or do could budge him from his stubborn resolve. Finally, James, his father, a skilled stonemason, decided Leonard could work with him on jobs around the area, and eventually Leonard became a productive member of the community, even though he never learned to read and write.

James, his brothers and his father, William Pedigo Tanner, were farmers, but they specialized in building structures, fences, stonemasonry and concrete work. Leonard learned to sign his name and, ironically, came to be a skilled mathematician, able to solve complicated formulas and engineering problems in his head. "Ol' Len may not be able to read or write," locals would say, "but he can cipher more in his head than most school teachers can on paper." James was proud of his once-blind son; he could give him the dimensions of a wood structure or a slab of concrete, and in a few minutes Len would tell him how much material they would need.

In Pea Ridge, many of the inhabitants made whiskey and corn liquor outside of the law. Len began drinking in his early teenage years and found himself at odds with his family and society in general on many occasions thereafter.

James Tanner (circa 1925)

Effie's parents had come to America from Ireland sometime after the Irish Potato Famine of 1845-1852, in hopes of finding a better life. After arriving in America, rather than staying in one of the big cities of the Northeast, as most Irish immigrants did, they elected to travel west to Kansas. Effie Towery and her brother Oscar were born sometime during that exodus. When Effie was eight or nine years old, her father died. Her mother remarried a short time later and after three or four years of marriage and two additional children, she died as well. Effie and Oscar were left with a man who was not their father. Oscar, when he came of age, joined the United States Navy, and Effie married Leonard at the age of sixteen, while working as a housekeeper for his father, James.

On this day in 1913, the family returned home from the Independence Day picnic and found Effie attending to her newborn baby boy. Effie was nothing if not a tough, innovative, fearless pioneer woman. She had birthed four previous babies and knew the procedure. Fortunately, there had been no complications and she was able to attend to whatever issues that may have occurred during the birthing process alone.

Her two oldest daughters, Iva and Ruth, upon seeing Effie and the newborn baby, quickly ran to her aid. Leonard, bleary-eyed from the day's festivities, instructed their son Frank, who was four years old and Clarace, two years younger, to stay out of the way, while the older girls attended to their mother and the new baby. Effie eventually bore twelve children, never once visiting a doctor or going to a hospital. The new baby was named Rex, and two years later another boy, Morris, was born. Frank was four years older than Rex and by far Leonard's favorite. Leonard taught him as much as he could, as fast as he could. Locals were amazed at how Frank, at seven years old, could control the family's mule team and make them back the family's wagon

Leonard & Effie Tanner (circa 1925)

up to a loading dock when they went to the feed and general store for supplies.

Although they lived on a farm just outside Collinsville, Leonard was a far cry from being a farmer. He earned his livelihood by verbally contracting construction-type jobs from nearby farmers and townspeople. He was also in demand during the fall butchering season when the local residents butchered their livestock to provide meat for the winter. Leonard was especially adept at the killing process, which many of the farmers found distasteful. Leonard, who was a powerfully built man, around 6 feet tall and 200 pounds, would grab a small sledgehammer, walk up to a distracted hog, which sometimes weighed more than 600 pounds, and deliver a lethal blow between the hog's eyes. Typically the hog would fall dead and Frank, even at 10 years old, would quickly cut the hog's throat with the Barlow knife Leonard had given him, and the other men would drag it to the slaughtering shed. Leonard seldom missed his mark, which was a large part of his value to the process, as it was a terrible distraction and quite dangerous to be chasing a wounded 600 pound hog around a small corral.

A popular but unsubstantiated tale was that on one occasion someone took Leonard's hammer and he became so angry that he walked up to the designated hog and killed it by hitting it between the eyes with his fist. Another favorite yarn about Leonard was that he once fought the town bully from early morning 'til "dinner time," sat down and ate lunch with him and resumed fighting after their repast until the early afternoon, whereupon, physically exhausted, both men mutually declared the altercation a draw and shared a pint of moonshine before they went home to their families.

Leonard depended heavily on Frank, much like his father James had leaned on him. Besides the two mules, the family didn't have any livestock. They bought milk from a neighbor and raised chickens for table meat and eggs. The

Daisy

various cuts of pork that Leonard took in payment for butchering and whatever fresh fruit and vegetables they could grow or for which they could trade, kept Effie's table sufficiently supplied. Rex and Morris did the outside chores, carrying water from the well in a bucket, going for milk, feeding and killing chickens when needed, gathering eggs and whatever other "manly" tasks that were required. They were commissioned to clean up the mule manure, but the mules were strictly Frank's responsibility and he tended to them religiously.

Tanner Children (circa 1919)
Left to right: Clarace, Effie May, Morris, Rex, Louise, Frank (note cigarette in left hand) and Juanita (in tub in foreground)

2

The Great Cover up

When Rex and Morris were ten and eight years old respectively, an incident occurred that put them at odds with Frank, which was a place most of the siblings strongly preferred not to be. Someone had given Leonard two Airedale puppies in payment for some work he and Frank had done. Rex and Morris were home all day, every day. The puppies, which they named Red and Curly, grew into strong adult dogs and upon command would do anything the boys had trained them to do. One thing they had trained them to do was hunt. No one had told them, if anyone even knew, that Airedales had been bred to hunt bear. Typically, eight to a dozen Airedales will track and corner a bear and fight the bear until they kill it, even while losing members of their pack in the fight. There are stories of Airedales, mortally wounded, even with their entrails protruding and dragging behind them, continuing to attack with the

pack until the bear was overcome or they died in battle, giving their last ounce of energy to the fight and their pack. It was easy to teach these dogs to chase and kill opossums, rabbits and squirrels, which often became the evening's supper. Foxes and raccoons were more difficult, but still not much of a challenge for Red and Curly. On one particular occasion the boys were out "hunting," when Morris saw what he took to be a wild razorback hog near a stand of hickory trees on a hill a couple of hundred yards away.

"Look Rex!" Morris exclaimed. "There's a wild hog up in that stand of trees."

Rex, also believing he was seeing a wild hog, without hesitation, cried, "Git 'em, Red; sic 'em, Curly," whereupon the dogs, who had by now picked up the scent of the wild boar, bolted forward, running pell-mell straight for the hog. The dogs quickly outdistanced the boys and by the time the boys breathlessly arrived at the scene, the hog lay gasping for his last breath, his throat having been torn out by one of the dogs.

"Jesus Christ," exclaimed Morris, "that's Woodrow Wilson, Jed Thacker's prize breed hog."

"Shit-fahr, Morris," answered Rex breathlessly, "what's that ugly piece of pork doin' out here in these woods?"

"Whatever it was," said Morris, "we're in about as much trouble as he is…I reckon maybe more, 'cause he's gone on to hog heaven by now. What are we gonna do?"

"Well, we cain't tell nobody what happened," counseled Rex, " 'cause, if we do, they'll kill Red and Curly for sure."

"And who knows what they'll do to us?" added Morris.

Rex began to think how best to resolve the situation. They could risk the dogs and tell Leonard, whereupon they would probably be flogged soundly and the dogs put down, but the meat from the hog could be salvaged, or they could come up with a plan where the hog disappeared and no one would ever know what happened. Ten year old Rex thought long and hard. Most probably, no one would believe the hog was taken by "hog rustlers," as the animal was too large. Wolves and cougars would leave a carcass behind, and a well-fed breed hog would hardly wander off looking for greener pastures.

"We're gonna bury 'im!" Rex announced.

"Bury 'im?" Morris challenged. "Shit, Rex, it'd take all day to dig a hole that big, and how are we gonna git 'im in the hole after we dig it?"

"It don't git dark 'til late and Dad and Frank won't be back 'til nearly dark. I reckon we can dig it in plenty of time, git 'im in it and cover his fat ass up 'fore anyone notices he's gone."

"But the son of a bitch is the fattest God damn hog this side of the Arkansas River. We'll never be able to move 'im an inch, much less roll 'im in the hole,"

"That's why we're hitchin' up the mules," Rex explained.

Rex knew it was risky using Frank's mules. If he found out and they located the hog grave site, Frank would probably thrash him and Morris mercilessly. Add to that Leonard's propensity to get drunk when a crisis occurred, and his exaggerated family pride and embarrassment over what had happened might ignite a situation that could rapidly spin out of control. Rex was committed to hiding what had happened, and the boys walked to the barn to get some shovels and hitch the mules to the wagon.

"We'll have to load whatever dirt that's left over on the wagon and take it a mile or two away; otherwise, someone'll just walk up, see where we was diggin' and just uncover the son of a bitch," counseled Rex.

"I reckon that's pretty smart. I just hope we got

enough time to do all this shit."

"We'll git 'er done," Rex promised. "Otherwise our asses might end up hangin' up on the shit-house wall, with some of them rattlesnakes we kilt."

The mules were hitched, the hole was dug, the hog was trussed with a makeshift rope harness and tied to the rear of the wagon, and then he was dragged into the hole. Rex, a very precocious ten year old boy, had wisely dug the hole on the downhill side of the hog so that when the wagon was backed up to the other side and the rope tied, the load was moving downhill. Once the payload was delivered into the hole, the rope harness was removed and the boys shoveled furiously, filling both hole and wagon. A mile or so away, the excess dirt was spread inconspicuously, and the boys returned to the barn and cleaned the residual dirt from the wagon with an old homemade straw broom. The mules were put back in their corral, the wagon in the barn and the shovels in the tool shed.

When Leonard and Frank returned home--luckily, for Rex and Morris, they had been riding back and forth to work with another crew of workers, which allowed the boys access to the mules and wagon--they went about whatever business they usually did before supper. Frank went out to feed the mules. Suddenly a few moments later he appeared at the entryway door.

"Rex! You and Morris come out here for a minute," he commanded.

Rex was engaged with setting the water bucket on the kitchen counter and pouring water into the ceramic bowl that the family dipped water from with a gourd, so Morris got to Frank first.

"Who's been foolin' with my mules?" Frank demanded to know.

"Shit-fahr, Frank, nobody I know'd fool around with anything of yourn."

"Them mules have been worked and that wagon don't look like it's where I remember leavin' it last time I drove it."

"Somebody left the gate unclasped and the mules got out," Rex offered as he walked up to join in the conversation. "Me 'n' Morris had to round 'em up and git 'em back in the corral. That's why they look like they been worked."

"Are you sayin' I left the gate open and the mules got out?" Frank challenged.

"Naw, I ain't sayin' nothin' like that…shit-fahr, Frank, maybe they bumped up ag'in' it and accidentally opened it their own selves," Rex answered.

"What about the wagon?" said Frank.

"I don't know nothin' 'bout the wagon; maybe the old man moved it for some reason," replied Rex.

Frank looked at Rex suspiciously. He knew something didn't add up. No harm seemed to have been done, so he wouldn't bother Leonard with it; besides he considered the mules to be his and he didn't think Leonard could handle his business or his younger brothers as well as he could.

"You boys leave them God damn mules alone when I'm gone," Frank instructed. "Otherwise I'm gonna come home and kick the shit out of both of you."

"We never come around them mules," Rex replied. "Jesus Christ, Frank, them mules won't pull for nobody but you, anyway. I wouldn't even try to hitch 'em to a wagon, for fear they'd kick my damn head off. Lucky as hell we uz able to git 'em back in the pen."

Rex's psychology seemed to resolve Frank's irritation and the three of them walked to the kitchen table to partake of Effie's hearty country supper of ham, fried chicken, beans, cornbread, greens, fried potatoes and butter that she churned by bouncing a Mason jar of raw cream on her thigh while she rocked in a rocking chair when she was taking a break from her household duties.

A few days later Leonard came home and mentioned that "Woodrow Wilson" had apparently escaped from his pen and wandered off and perhaps "some Indians" had found him and butchered him.

Leonard Garth "Buster" Tanner

3

Bull Dog / Bull Durham

Leonard's brother Fayette had prayed for Leonard to regain his sight and was convinced that his prayers had been answered. Leonard was two years younger than Fayette, and they remained very close until their middle years. Fayette had followed his heart and, along with his wife, became a Pentecostal preacher. In addition to their second-oldest son Buster, born in 1901 in Oklahoma Indian Territory, they had a younger son, Kilmer, born in Indian Territory as well in 1903, and another son, Elwood, born in 1912, who was a year older than Rex. Fayette and his wife lived in Claremore with their other children, a few miles away from Leonard and his family.

Occasionally, Kilmer or Elwood would "stay over" for a couple of days at their Uncle Leonard's. Buster, like the other Tanner men, made his livelihood doing concrete and masonry work and like Leonard's part-time butchering service, Buster broke wild horses for ranchers around the area. Buster was an authentic, good-natured, rough and tumble Oklahoma cowboy. Sometimes on the weekends he would participate in bare-knuckle boxing matches, usually knocking his opponent unconscious early in the fight. He gradually took charge of the family's construction work business as Fayette became increasingly committed to becoming a full-time preacher. Elwood wasn't much interested in interacting with Rex and Morris, even though he was near their age. When he came to visit, he would try to keep as much distance between him and them as possible. Rex and Morris ignored him. Their life was filled with adventure and activity and a stick-in-the-mud like Elwood could not dampen their enthusiasm for the day's unfolding events.

"You better watch them boys, Elwood," Kilmer would say when Elwood was unduly rude or disrespectful to them. "There's two of them and they're rough as a cob; only one of you and they're liable to double up and whoop yer ass."

The boys liked Kilmer, who was six years older than their brother Frank, even though they knew that Kilmer had a reputation for being mean, aggressive and dangerous. A year or two before the "The Great Cover-up," Kilmer had shown up at their farm while Leonard and Frank were away working.

"How far's that country store down the road?" inquired Kilmer.

"I reckon it's prob'ly about three or four miles," responded Rex.

"I ain't got nary a smoke; here's a dollar," said Kilmer. "Why'nt you boys walk on down there and git me a carton of Camel tailor-made cigarettes and you can keep the change and I'll give you a pack, too?"

"We'd rather have a sack of Bull Durham and some rollin' papers," replied Morris. "Trouble is, there's a bulldog about halfway there and we can sneak past 'im, but once he knows we've come by, he waits for us to come back. He's bit a few people and the old farmer down there won't tie 'im up or git rid of 'im. He says he don't want nobody walkin' past his house anyway, fearin' they might steal somethin' and he thinks it's funny when the bulldog gits after people."

"So how do you git past 'im on the way back?" Kilmer inquired.

"That's the problem," said Rex. "We have to go a mile or two down a side road and another couple of miles back this way, then walk through the brush a mile or two, lookin' out for rattlesnakes, to git back here."

"Tell you what, boys," Kilmer responded, "y'all go on and git past that bulldog and I'll make sure he don't bother you comin' back. Come to think of it," Kilmer added, "here's another quarter and you can buy your Bull Durham and rollin' papers and I'll still give you a pack of the tailor-mades…and you can keep whatever change there is."

Rex and Morris cautiously approached the property where the bulldog lived. As they passed, the bulldog picked up their scent and ran to the road to attack them. It wasn't difficult to outrun the bulldog once they were halfway in front of his owner's property; like Rex had said, it was getting back that was the problem.

The boys got their tobacco and Kilmer's cigarettes, along with some candy and soda pop with the extra money Kilmer had given them. They weren't sure about returning the way they had come, but Kilmer had said he'd make sure it was safe and they believed and trusted him. As they approached the bulldog's property, they cautiously and carefully stepped lightly, so as not to arouse him, all the while keeping a sharp eye out for him coming on the run. Halfway past the farm house there was no sign of the bulldog.

They were nearly past the property when Morris glanced to his left, away from the bull dog's home and ex-

Daisy

claimed, "Jesus Christ, Rex…look at that!"

Across from the farmer's property was the bulldog, throat cut, cut open under the rib cage and impaled on a fence post, grinning sardonically, with his eyes rolled back in his head.

"Shit!" exclaimed Rex. "Ol Kilmer wasn't shittin' when he told us he'd take care of that bulldog."

"I wonder if he did that without gittin' dog-bit?" pondered Morris. "I reckon we'll find out in a few minutes."

"Hey boys," Kilmer greeted them, apparently dog-bite free, when they returned. "Did you git my cigarettes?"

"Yeah Kilmer," Rex said, "and the fixin's fer roll yer owns, too."

"You didn't see that bulldog, did you…on the way back?" asked Kilmer.

"Naw, we didn't see 'im. He wasn't around this time when we come back," Rex lied.

Kilmer nonchalantly opened up a pack of his tailor-mades and pulled one out and lit it. "Reckon ol' Len and Frank'll be comin' home dreckly," he said. "Y'all better git to gittin' Effie whatever she needs to git dinner on the table."

Kilmer took a long pull off the Camel cigarette and gazed out the window; he was eighteen years old and just beginning on a road of crime and violence that would eventually land him in the federal penitentiary at Leavenworth, Kansas.

Kilmer Tanner (circa 1921)

4

Red Headed Stranger

"Hey…mah nime's Homuh Caawcks, from Blacksveal Joe-ja; whatcha all up tew 'round heah?" The red-haired, freckle-faced boy walking toward Rex and Morris looked to be somewhere in the vicinity of their age.

"Who you, boy, and where the hell is Blacksveal Joe-ja?" said Morris.

"I reckon he means 'Georgia'," said Rex. "That right, Homer?"

"That's what I say-ed, Joe-ja…we all just moved ee-un at the ol' Bradford fawm 'bout a mall awaiy frum heah."

"Oh yeah," said Rex, "they useta have a mean ol' bull dog lived there."

"Naw, ain't no bulldog there now, least none I seen."

"How old'r you, boy?" Morris asked.

"Aum nan year old, soon to be teeun; how old'r

ya'll?"

The boy was about the same age as Morris. Morris ignored his question and continued, "How much you weigh?"

"I don't rightly know but my daddy says I'm prob'ly 'bout foe foot nan inches…maybe talluh."

"I didn't know they stacked shit that high," Morris said. "You 'bout an ugly little red-haired shit-heel."

Rex laughed and Homer Cox smiled slightly. Morris loved a good joke and he instinctively recognized Homer Cox's potential as a good material source.

"Whatta y'all do 'round heah when y'aint doin' chouz?" said Homer.

"We got these slingshots and we hunt possums, rabbits and squirrels with our dogs," said Morris. "Sometimes we even hunt wild razorback hogs."

"No sheeut?" said Homer. "They's wild hogs 'round heah?"

"Shore is, Red," Morris continued. "We saw one once on the other side of that draw over yonder."

"Y'all ever shoot mawbles?" Red asked.

"Sure, when we used to go to school, 'fore the neighbor that took us moved away, we'd play all the time at school. Rex was the marble champion of the whole damn school."

"Wail, ah got me some mawbles and I kin shoot some, mahself," said Homer. "Maybe we all kin have us some mawble games."

"Next time ya come, go ahead and bring 'em," said Rex. "I don't mind takin' 'em from you."

"Wail, we'll just have ta see 'bout thayut," said Homer.

Homer began to visit the boys often. Although he lost all his marbles the first day, he loved roaming the fields and scaring up squirrels and rabbits with the Tanner boys. Rex made him a slingshot from the fork of a hickory tree limb. He cut rubber strands from an old inner tube that Frank had brought home from a job and tied them to a pouch that he made from the tongue of an old shoe. He tied the rubber strands to the perfectly shaped hickory fork with heavy twine that Leonard kept in the barn for laying out block walls. The boy's slingshots were surprisingly accurate. When they could procure heavy buckshot for ammunition, they used that; otherwise, they mostly used rocks and whatever old metal particles they could scare up. For a few hours they used Homer's marbles. Sometimes they would get bored and playfully shoot at each other. On those occasions they took dry beans from the family's food storage shed, keeping a sharp eye out for Effie, and used those.

One day Homer came walking up to the house with what appeared to be a rifle.

"Jesus, Homer," Morris said, "who give ya that gun?"

"It's a BB gun, Mawis. My daddy got it for me for mah birthday."

"Let me see," said Rex. "I reckon we can go shootin' some birds or somethin'."

Homer had brought plenty of BBs and the boys spent most of the afternoon shooting at various targets, including some in flight.

"Hey, I got an idea," said Rex. "Kilmer give me a .22 bullet a while back. Let me show you boys somethin'."

Rex got the bullet and explained to Morris and Homer how the firing pin of a firearm breaks the primer at the rear of a bullet, exploding the cap, which ignites the gun powder and propels the lead slug forward.

"Here's what we'll do," said Rex. "We'll put the bullet up on a fence post, point it at a target and try to shoot it and break the primer with the BB gun and see if it hits the target."

What a wonderful idea, the other two boys thought, and the three of them began to take turns trying to be the one that hit the "bull's eye." They started out from a distance of

about 20 feet. No "bull's eyes" were forthcoming and they began to move closer to the target. When they were six to eight feet from the bullet, Rex hit the bull's eye. The bullet fired, as they had hoped, but rather than the lead slug going forward and hitting the target, the casing flew backward and lodged in Homer's face, between his right nostril and his upper lip.

"Ahm shot! Oh shit, Ahm shot!" Homer screamed. "Jesus Christ, ahm gonna die fo' sho-uh."

Homer began to run for home, but before he could reach the road, Rex tackled him.

"Grab that Barlow outta my back pocket, Morris," he instructed. "We cain't let 'im go home with a bullet in his face…shit, his ol' man'll kill him and us both."

Homer was nearly hysterical. Rex held him firmly and calmed him down enough to inspect the wound. "Shit-fahr, Morris, it ain't no bullet in his lip; it's the casing."

"It don't mattuh," cried Homer, "ah gotta go find mah daddy."

"Yo' daddy is about the last thing we need 'round here right now…Morris, I'll hold 'im still, you take that Barlow and dig that casing outta there. Homer, you lay still or I'm gonna have to knock you out."

Homer obeyed as best he could. He could feel and taste the blood running in his mouth and dripping from his face. Morris carefully extracted the .22 casing from above his lip, and Rex took his red railroad handkerchief and pressed it against the wound to help stop the bleeding.

"Gawd Dayumn, Ray-ex, what am ah gonna tail mah daddy?"

"Well, you ain't gonna tell 'im I shot you with a damn .22 bullet…are you shittin' me? Just tell 'im you tripped and fell on some bob wahr and it ripped your damn lip open."

"Oh Gawd," Homer lamented, "ain't no pretty gal ever gonna wanna kee-us me now."

"Well, for Christ's sake, you homely little redheaded shit-ass," Morris said, "they warn't no pretty gal ever gonna kiss your ugly mug, anyway."

When Homer regained his composure, Rex laid out the story they would all stick to, if questioned. Homer went home with his BB gun and never returned. Apparently he had been able to convince his daddy that it had been an accident involving a barbed wire fence, and no one ever mentioned the incident to the boys. Two weeks later the Tanner boys and their family moved to Claremore.

5

Claremore

Moving from the idyllic country life outside Collinsville to the more densely populated Claremore area was a bit of an adjustment for Rex. He sorely missed the independence he enjoyed each day when Leonard and Frank left early in the morning and didn't return until dusk and he was free to explore the countryside with Morris and the dogs. Rex was barely thirteen and besides his older sisters Iva, Ruth and Clarace, Effie had given birth to Effie Mae, Louise, Juanita and Pearl. With Leonard and Frank gone most of the time, Rex and Morris had to contend with eight females.

The first week, Leonard suggested Rex join him and Frank on a job they were doing for a local business. At the end of the week Leonard collected the twelve dollars that the three of them had earned and when he came to settle up, he gave Rex fifty cents and split the remainder with Frank. Rex was almost grown by now, at least physically, and he worked hard to try to stay up with Frank, to impress his father, Leonard. Frank was embarrassed but didn't say anything. Leonard was oblivious and focused his attention on where he was going to find a bottle of liquor to get him through the weekend. When Leonard walked away, Rex flipped the fifty-cent piece Leonard had given him to Frank and walked home. On the way home he passed a vacant field where a group of teenage boys were playing football.

"Hey kee-ud," shouted one of the boys, "ya'll ever played football?"

"Naw," Rex answered, "never even seen it before."

"Hell, it ain't hard, boy. Ya just take the ball and try to git from one end of the field to the other and the other team tries to tackle you. Come own! We're a player short; we'll show ya what to do."

The boys appeared to be a couple of years older than Rex, although most of them were around his size. Rex was dispatched to the team opposing the boy who had invited him to play and was told to block whoever tried to come through from the left side of scrimmage. The boy who had invited him was playing behind the defensive right side lineman, who Rex was instructed to block. When the play was completed, Rex, having blocked his man, turned and stood looking at the pile of boys who had been involved in the play. Rex suddenly felt himself hit from behind and driven savagely into the ground.

"Shit, Chester," one of the boys said, "you like to of tore his God damn head off. He wasn't even in the play."

"That's football, kee-ud," Chester said. "It ain't no game for sissies."

Rex slowly got to his feet. He had fallen awkwardly on his right arm and it was broken between the shoulder and elbow. His arm dangled rather oddly and he was in intense pain. He slowly walked toward Chester, who was grinning arrogantly and chuckling at the other boys, and when he got within range, Rex brought his right foot up swiftly between Chester's legs, striking him solidly in the crotch. Chester's eyes bulged as he absorbed the kick and quickly bent over in pain. Rex then brought his right knee up suddenly and made solid contact with Chester's left cheekbone. Chester went down and began rolling on the ground. Rex, with his right arm dangling, tried to pummel him with his left arm until the other boys surrounded him and forced him to stop.

"What's wrong with you, boy?" someone said. "We oughta kick the shit out of you fer what you just done to Chester."

"Well, I reckon y'all better go ahead and break my other arm, then, and prob'ly my legs, too, and then I'm goin' to crawl on into town and bring back Kilmer and Frank Tanner and my brother Morris and we're gonna kick the shit out of all you football playin' assholes."

The mood changed abruptly when Kilmer and Frank were mentioned and someone said, "Well, I reckon we prob'ly didn't explain the rules good enough and he ain't never played football before and Chester prob'ly shouldn't have hit 'im from the back like he did. Maybe we should just call it even and go on home and forget about playin' football today."

Rex, grimacing in pain, was holding his broken arm while staying in position to kick whoever ventured toward him. He had learned to kick from having to defend himself from Frank when they were young boys. In those days, Morris would usually join him and most times whatever disagreement there was would end in a standoff. There was no Morris this day, and Rex was drawing on his rather remarkable ingenuity, backing off ten or so older boys with the threat of reinforcements. It didn't hurt that the reinforcements included Kilmer Tanner, who had become notorious locally from some of his outrageous behavior.

Rex glanced at Chester and asked, "Are we done?"

Chester was sitting up, holding his swollen cheekbone. He nodded affirmatively and Rex backed up several paces, turned and briskly walked away. His broken arm was swollen to twice its size by now, and he knew something would have to be done to mend it. A block or so away from the football field, another boy approached him. The boy looked to be three or four years older than Rex, probably around Frank's age.

"I seen what them boys did to you," the new boy said. "I liked what you did back, too," he added.

Rex glanced at him, but didn't answer.

"Hey, ain't you one of them Tanner boys?"

"I reckon I am," Rex replied.

"Hell yeah, I remember you from over in Collinsville. You're the one your ol' daddy put up to recite that poem about the Kaiser when you was a little kid."

"I remember that," Rex said, "I didn't know what it meant, still don't, but I remember all the men havin' a big laugh after I said it."

"Do you remember how it went?" the boy asked.

"Sure I do: God made the white man, the devil made the Jew...whoever made the Kaiser had but damn little to do."

"Yeah, that was it," the boy said. "The Kaiser was the head of the Germans when we was fightin' the world war."

"Well, what's a Jew?" Rex asked.

"I reckon they're people that have lots of money and own banks and such. My name's Jack Burns...are you Rex?"

"I'm Rex...So what do Jews look like?"

"I think they're about the same as us...prob'ly smarter," said Jack.

"Are there any in Claremore?"

"I don't rightly know," said Jack. "Maybe one owns the bank or somethin'."

"Well, how did they git to be Jews?" asked Rex.

"I think they killed Jesus, or maybe it was Moses… hell, I don't know. They got lots of money, though,"

"Maybe I'll try to be a Jew," said Rex. "I'd like to have lots of money."

Jack laughed and continued, "We better git you to ol' Doc Simpson and git that arm set…reckon you don't really need it all that much, though, bein' able to kick like you do."

As they were nearing the doctor's office, Kilmer came out of a store front and saw the boys. Kilmer was about twenty-three years old and townspeople avoided him like the plague.

"What happened to you, Rex?" he asked.

"Well, some boys asked me to play football and one of them assholes broke my arm on the first play and I got up and whipped his ass with my other arm and now I'm fixin' to go to Doc Simpson's with my new friend Jack Burns, here."

"I'm right proud to know you, Kilmer...I seen the whole thing as I was walkin' up," said Jack. "Rex backed down the whole lot of 'em, with his right arm hangin'."

"How'd you do that?" asked Kilmer.

"Well, they come-inse makin' a circle around me and sayin' they was gonna whip my ass and I told 'em I'd bring you 'n' Frank 'n' Morris and we-ud whoop all their football playin' asses." Then Rex added, "I told 'em if they didn't like that I kicked their friend in the nuts that THEIR nuts might end up hangin' on a fencepost if we all took a notion to come back."

Kilmer was caught by surprise and laughed heartily. Rex and Morris had never admitted to anyone that they had seen the bulldog on the fence post five years earlier. Kilmer liked it that Rex and Morris kept their business private and to themselves; that was his style and Frank's, too. Rex's style was to surprise you with something you didn't expect at an opportune moment.

Leaving Kilmer, Rex and Jack were walking the rest of the way to Doc Simpson's when Jack questioned Rex about the bulldog reference.

"Me 'n' Morris had to run past a bulldog at our place over in Collinsville to git Kilmer some cigarettes. He told us he'd make sure the coast was clear when we come back and when we did the bulldog was throat-cut and split open over a fence post," Rex said.

"Jesus, Rex...that Kilmer's a mean son of a bitch, ain't he?"

"I reckon if you're a bulldog he is," said Rex.

"I'm thinkin' he don't like dogs a'tall," said Jack. "Prob'ly people neither."

"Why do you say that?" Rex asked.

"Well, they say he had this gal friend 'cross town that dropped 'im for an ol' boy that worked at the post office. She had this little cur dog that she carried around with her ever'where she went. The dog and Kilmer got along OK when she was his girlfriend, but after she throwed 'im over, Kilmer was walkin' past her house one day and the dog run out and tried to bite 'im. Somebody said Kilmer got holt of the dog, flipped 'im around and cut his damn head off."

"Christ," said Rex, "I reckon it ain't just bulldogs he don't like...so what happened next?"

"Well, he taken the dog and throwed it and his head up on her porch and went on about his business...But that ain't the end of it."

"What else?" asked Rex.

"Then a couple of weeks later he follows the ex-girlfriend and her new beau out to the country where they're tryin' to have a picnic. He walks up, throws a gun on 'em and takes all their money and some jewelry he'd bought her. Then he takes the ol' boy's keys and drives off in his car, leavin' them afoot."

"He had a gun?" asked Rex.

"That's what they're a sayin', AND they're sayin' he drove the car to Tulsa and sold it and kept the money."

"Shit-fahr, boy, that's plumb stupid; I never woulda thought Kilmer'd do somethin' like that."

"That ain't all of it, neither," Jack went on. "They're sayin' a short time later he walked by a couple of ol' boys from the telephone company who was up on a platform fixin' some wahrs and he saw the keys in their truck and hopped in and stole their truck while they was up a pole, workin' on the damn phone lines."

"I wonder how he could git away with somethin' like that," said Rex, "shit-fahr…our uncle Elmer's the Chief of Police."

"Maybe that's how he gits away with it," replied Jack. "Mostly, though, I think it's just that folks are afraid of 'im and hope if they don't say nothin', he'll leave 'em alone."

"What did he do with the phone truck?" asked Rex.

"Prob'ly took it to the same place as the ol' boy's car, over in Tulsa,"

The boys were at the doctor's office by now. Rex and Jack went in and the doctor examined Rex and diagnosed a simple fracture that would require he wear a cast for a few weeks. Rex returned home to convalesce, knowing he wouldn't be joining Leonard and Frank for a while. He knew inside, though, that he wasn't going to work for Leonard again, and he began to plan what he should do when his arm healed. While Rex's arm was mending, he and Jack spent many hours and days familiarizing Rex with Claremore. Rex had heard people refer to Will Rogers but didn't really know who he was or much about him. Jack told him about Will being a world famous personality and that he lived over in Ooligah, a few miles north of Claremore.

"When ol' Will's not out explorin' the world or makin' movies, he stays at his ranch…sometimes he comes to the Post Office and everybody gathers 'round and he tells stories about his journeys and people he's met," Jack said.

"I think my daddy and Uncle Fayette know 'im," said Rex. "Fer sure Elmer knows 'im."

"He ought to; hell, he's the Chief of Police," said Jack.

6

Junkyard Dogs

Rex knew if he was going to avoid working with Leonard, he was going to have to find a job of some kind. He had made up his mind that when he could sustain himself financially, he would move out of the house and relieve Effie of the burden of one more mouth to feed. Leonard's drinking had become even more of a negative influence on the family with the move to town. Frank, now seventeen, had bought a used Model T Ford car and rented his own room at a boarding house, and word around town was that he was supplementing his wages by bootlegging whiskey when Leonard was too drunk or hung-over to work. Frank had made friends with the owner of the only taxi stand in Claremore and sometimes dispatched cabs during the late evening and early morning hours.

Since his early childhood Frank had carried a Barlow knife. No one ever saw it, with the exception of when he was butchering hogs with Leonard. Frank, when asked to lend it, always replied, "I don't own a knife." Frank's knife was a five-inch single blade model that he kept honed razor sharp. He had given Rex his old knife, a shorter bladed Barlow about three inches long when Rex was eight years old. Rex wasn't much interested in knives and except for digging .22 casings out of neighbor boy's lips, hardly ever used it. Kilmer always carried a knife and didn't care who knew it. If confronted he would immediately put his hand in his front pocket, an implied warning, much like an Oklahoma rattlesnake letting you know not to come closer or suffer the consequences. Jack Burns wasn't a fighter and he wasn't mean and wouldn't even dream of carrying a weapon of any kind. Rex had long since lost his Barlow and when asked to lend his knife would reply, "Hell, I ain't carried a knife since I got big enough to kill a man with my fists."

During Rex's convalescence, Jack told him about a junkyard that sustained itself by scrapping metal from the nearby oil fields and dismantling and salvaging parts from wrecked cars and wagons. Together they visited the place and engaged the owner in conversation, and Rex asked him for a job.

"You Len Tanner's boy?" Fred, the owner, asked.

"Reckon I am," replied Rex. "I'm lookin' fer work so's I kin move out on my own."

"Well, I'm proud to know you, son. I've knowed ol' Len fer years; he used to call square dances down at the Mason's Hall some years back...he's a good ol' boy. They say he once kilt a full growed hog with his fist."

"I don't know if that's a true story," replied Rex, "but he kin sure as hell kill one with a sledge hammer."

Fred laughed. "He likes his whiskey, too," Fred continued. "Not too many ol' boys 'round these parts kin keep up with 'im."

"I reckon that's true. That's one reason why it's time

I need to move on."

"Well, I tell ya what, son…soon as you git shut of that cast on yer arm, y'all come on back and I'll pay you a dollar a day and you kin stay in that bunkhouse over yonder fer nothin'. Yer on yer own far as meals go and sometimes there's other fellas stay in the bunkhouse. Right now there's not, but it'll accommodate four men."

"I'll take the job," said Rex, "and you won't be sorry; I'm a good hand and I kin drive a car iffen need be."

Rex had learned to drive when friends and relatives would come to visit the farm in Collinsville. It was generally accepted by most that if you drove a car to see Leonard and Effie, much of the time you were there, Rex and Morris would be driving up and down the road in your car

"Well, shore nuff," said Fred. "We got some ol' trucks 'round here that we use to haul stuff around. You'd be surprised how many folks nowadays ain't learned how to drive."

"Well, I kin drive and I kin work, and how 'bout I start the beginning of next week?" asked Rex.

"Next week it is, Rex; we'll be lookin' forward to seein' you."

"All right, then," answered Rex, "I'll git up with the roosters and be here bright 'n' early."

When Rex returned home he announced to the family that he had found a job and would be moving out. Leonard hadn't been home for several days and Frank was living in town and working at nights at the taxi stand. Morris wasn't thrilled to hear the news, but he had been helping Leonard on jobs and at eleven years old, the fifty cents that Leonard paid him each day satisfied him for the time being.

"You reckon I could git a job over where yer goin'?" Morris asked.

"Let me make a hand first and then we'll try to git you on over there," Rex replied.

"Yeah, anyway, with you and Frank both gone, somebody needs to be here and watch out for Mama and the girls," Morris said.

Rex moved to the junkyard and learned the process of scrapping metal and dismantling old vehicles to sell their components as replacement parts. He had a natural mechanical bent and was energetic and intelligent. Workers came and went; some stayed in the bunkhouse for a while and some just came to work like any other job.

About two years after Rex had begun his employment there, a big slow-witted man about thirty years old came to work and took residence in the bunkhouse. There wasn't anyone else besides Rex living there at the time, and Rex had never had a problem getting along with any of the previous tenants. One day Morris came to work for a couple of days, as he often did by now, and some kind of disagreement developed between the slow-witted man and Morris. Morris, who had developed a razor sharp wit, called the man a "half-wit." Rex interceded on Morris's behalf and the slow-witted man seemed to accept the reconciliation terms that Rex had laid out. After Rex and Morris had fallen asleep that night, Rex awoke to someone sitting astride him punching him in the face. Every time a blow landed, Rex would see flashes of light.

"Morris! Git this son of a bitch off me!" Rex screamed.

Morris awoke and jumped from the top bunk where he was sleeping to the floor and saw the shadow of the half-wit pummeling Rex with his fists. The half-wit was a large slow-moving man, but the element of surprise and the strength of his position on top of Rex gave him tremendous advantage. Morris punched the half-wit in the side of the head, but it hardly fazed him. He then grabbed him by the hair and tried to dislodge him from Rex, but that failed too. By now Rex had been hit fifteen or twenty times in the face and could hardly make out the half-wit's form in the darkened room. Morris finally located a brass spittoon that the workers used for discharging their chewing tobacco and swung it broadly, connecting with the half-wit's forehead. That seemed to stun him momentarily, and Morris swung and connected again. The half-wit fell slightly to one side and Rex was able to get from beneath him. Together, like the Airedales, they punched, kicked and stomped until the half-wit, knocked senseless by now, retreated into the night. The boys followed the half-wit outside, but he ran away and apparently hid among the scrap and rubble of the junkyard.

Rex's eyes were swollen shut, his nose was broken and his lips were bleeding. Amazingly, his teeth were intact and his jaw, though bruised, wasn't broken. Morris led him by the hand and together they walked the few miles home to Leonard and Effie's. Leonard was gone, as might have been expected, but Effie and the girls dressed Rex's wounds as best they could and Rex went to see Doc Simpson the next day.

"Hang on there, boy," Doc Simpson said as he prepared to set Rex's nose, "what I'm fixin' to do is gonna hurt like hell."

It did and Rex grimaced in pain.

"You didn't start a fight with your cousin Buster, did you, son?" the doctor joked. "That ol' boy's sent me plenty of business over the years."

"Naw," Rex replied, "this was a half-wit over at the junkyard. This is the first time I ever got my ass whipped."

"If what you're sayin' about wakin' up with the son of a bitch sittin' on your chest, punchin' you in the face is accurate, I wouldn't call it much of an ass whoopin'," Doc Simpson countered. "I'd call it assault."

"Well, I'm here with you and he's out there someplace with a nose that prob'ly ain't broke, so I'm callin' it an ass whoopin' and until I catch up with 'im somewhere down the road, he won the fight."

When Rex returned to the junkyard to pick up his final paycheck, he didn't see the slow-witted gentleman. Fred pleaded with Rex to reconsider leaving his employ and said if the attacker ever showed up to collect the money Fred owed him, he'd have him arrested and charged with assault.

Rex was done and ready to move on. He was fifteen and looked and carried himself like a man five to ten years older. He'd been talking to Jack Burns about a trip to find gold in Mexico, an adventure that Rex was eager to pursue. Some months previously, Jack had saved his life from drowning in a nearby river when the current swept him downstream into rough water. Jack was an excellent swimmer and had jumped in and pulled Rex to safety using a broken tree branch to keep them both afloat. Rex trusted Jack and considered him to be his best friend.

Jack Burns

7

Mexican Gold

"I got a friend named Kelvin Hooks that says some ol' boy give 'im a map and some information about a river down in Mexico where you can pick gold nuggets out of some shallow places in the bends of the river and nobody down there knows about it."

Jack Burns had made this comment to Rex a few days before the "ass whoopin'."

"Sounds like a bird's nest on the ground, Jack; how do we git there?" Rex asked.

"Well, Kelvin wants to go and he says we need three men: two to pan the gold and one to stay in camp. He says it's pretty isolated and there ain't no people around...hell, we could prob'ly have enough gold for us all to be rich in a couple of weeks."

"Well, all right then, count me in...I wonder why no Mexicans know about it," said Rex.

"I don't think Mexicans care much about gold," said Jack. "It's so damn hot down there, they mostly sleep all afternoon, I hear."

"A little heat don't bother me," said Rex. "Over at the junkyard I'd put all them ol' boys in the shade when it got hot."

"Kelvin's got an old truck we kin use to haul our shit in…when we git a load of gold we kin just go ahead and leave all the shit we brought down there."

"What's a load of gold worth, anyway?" asked Rex.

"Shit, there's no tellin'…a lot, I'd think. I reckon we'll be livin' high on the hog when we git back."

Rex, at fifteen, was eager to make his mark in the world. Striking it rich panning gold in Mexico had an appeal to him that was beyond his grasp of probability. Jack was nineteen and Kelvin was in his mid-twenties. It took a week or so to outfit the truck and collect supplies for the trip. They planned to drive to Brownsville, Texas, in two or three days and then continue on to Mexico the next day. The map was fairly clear and cited major landmarks, but the distance wasn't readily discernible. They asked Leonard to try to cipher the distance by looking at the map, comparing it with an old atlas someone had given them. Leonard said their intended destination appeared to be somewhere between eighty and one hundred miles into Mexico from Brownsville, depending on the twists and turns of the road. All agreed they could probably drive to Brownsville in a couple of days and then leave Brownsville at dawn the next day and reach their destination by mid-afternoon. It was mid-summer, so the extended days gave them a bit of a cushion, if it indeed took longer than expected. Surprisingly, the journey was uneventful. The map proved fairly accurate and they found the location the map provider had cited.

It only took a couple of hours to unload the truck and set up camp. Spirits were high as they sat around the campfire and exchanged stories and planned what they would all do with their shares of the gold. The following day Kelvin and Jack set out for the river of gold nuggets. Rex prepared breakfast and stayed in camp, cleaning up and arranging their supplies more efficiently. When Kelvin and Jack returned in the late afternoon they had a small container of something that appeared to resemble gold.

"It ain't as easy as that ol' boy said," said Kelvin, "but if this is gold we at least have evidence that it's out there."

"It's gold all right," said Jack. "I've seen it before and that's what it looks like. We got to learn how to use them pans and the other stuff we bought better…we'll bring home a lot more tomorrow."

The second day did indeed bring better results. Kelvin and Jack returned to the camp exhausted but with what seemed to be a couple of ounces of gold.

"Hell, we prob'ly paid for our trip already," Jack speculated. "I'm thinkin' ever'day's gonna git a little better…it's damn hard work, though, not as easy as we expected."

The men retired early that night; the camp fire burned down to smoldering embers. At around midnight they were rudely awakened. At first Rex thought a bear or some other wild animal had ventured into their camp. A few passing moments brought the realization that they had been invaded not by wild animals, but by a group of a dozen or so Mexican banditos, armed with pistols, rifles and sabers. The gold prospectors were pushed together, wearing only the long johns that they had been sleeping in as the Mexicans ransacked their camp. In a few minutes it became apparent that if they remained calm, physical harm was unlikely. The Mexicans were laughing and joking amongst themselves as they took all the food, clothing, tools, matches and gasoline that the Americans had brought. Of course, they found the

gold, which caused them all to laugh heartily. The final humiliation came when as they were leaving, one of the Mexicans gathered up all their shoes and left the men barefooted and still wearing only their long handled underwear. It didn't take the Americans long to figure out their truck was worthless now, with no gasoline. It wasn't like they could replace the lost gasoline, even if they had managed to salvage some money…which they hadn't.

"What do we do now?" Jack wondered aloud.

"Looks to me like we got a long walk ahead of us," said Rex. "We better figure out a way to carry some water; it looked pretty damned dry on the way down here."

The Mexican bandits had left behind a few containers that had been discarded after their contents had been consumed at mealtime. Each man took the largest container he could carry and together, at dawn, they walked the short distance to the river and filled them with water. Then they began their long trek north, only to be stopped a short time later by the burning heat of the road upon which they were walking barefoot. It was late afternoon or early evening before the ground cooled enough for them to walk on it. Luckily, the moon was waxing, which allowed them to see well enough to continue walking along the road at night. They had encountered few vehicles during the day on the trip south and even fewer as they trekked north in the dark. Whenever a car did come upon them, it would slow down and its occupants would stare curiously at them and then speed up. In a couple of days hunger was becoming a major concern. They still had enough water for a day or two, but they were ravenous. A few times they ventured up to a ramshackle farm house and attempted to bargain for food. They had nothing to bargain with, but some of the residents took pity on them and offered them whatever they could spare. Some of the people allowed them to sleep in a barn or shed…a couple of times they were able to sneak into a chicken coop and procure a few eggs, which they cracked and consumed raw.

It took ten days to get back to Brownsville, and then they were shunned by most of the Americans they encountered because of their unshaven faces and bizarre dress. At least the Texans spoke their language and after telling their sad tale a few times, they found enough kindness and support to buy some cheap pants, shirts and shoes, share a razor blade and begin hitchhiking back to Oklahoma. It took almost as long to get back home as it did to get from the river back to Brownsville; not many would stop and offer a ride to three grubby looking ex-prospectors. One time they managed to board a freight train, only to find instead of continuing north, as they expected, it suddenly veered west and took them even farther from their desired destination before they could find an opportunity to jump off safely. Finally, after many jumps and starts, the three found Claremore's city limits, whose citizens were celebrating a local hero's victory in "The Great Intercontinental Foot Race," which was a marathon that ran from New York City to Los Angeles, California. Andy Payne from Foyil, Oklahoma, a few miles north of Claremore, had won the race and collected the $25,000 prize.

"I reckon ol' Andy had to walk a hell of a lot further'n we did," said Rex. "The other side of that, though, is he actually came home with some gold."

8

The World Champion Of The Mid-West

During the time Rex worked in the junkyard, before the Mexican adventure, he would spend many weekends and weekday evenings hanging around Claremore's downtown area, usually with Jack Burns. The local domino parlor was a popular hangout for many of the young men from the nearby oil fields, as well as some of the local residents. Since Jack was four years older than Rex, he naturally became somewhat of an influence on him regarding social and recreational pursuits. Radio had begun broadcasting from Tulsa in 1925 and developed programming sophistication as its popularity grew. Silent movies were popular and although Claremore had a modest theater, Tulsa had a more impressive venue, with a live theater organ that played during showings, enhancing the films greatly. Rex and Jack would sometimes board the daily freight train that stopped in

Claremore, Oklahoma

Claremore on its way to Tulsa. As the train began picking up speed, as it made the first turn out of Claremore, the engineer would lose sight of the rear cars and the boys and others had about a sixty-second opportunity to crawl up into an open boxcar without being seen.

It was a free forty-five minute ride to Tulsa and a return trip the next day, and all you had to do was keep track of the time and be agile enough to swing up onto a boxcar moving ten to fifteen miles an hour. The boys would entertain themselves in Tulsa by going to films, playing pool and dominos and listening to radio broadcasts at the pool hall.

Rex had a natural affinity for music and although he didn't sing much or play an instrument, he was an exceptional whistler. Jack told him about a famous whistler named Elmo Tanner, who made phonograph records, and after Rex had heard him whistle on a phonograph record, he began to imitate Elmo's style. Critics said that Elmo was able to achieve his unusually rich whistle tone by whistling from deep in his throat, using his larynx. Rex quickly discovered and copied the technique and became a source of entertainment for Jack and others who rode the boxcars into Tulsa. While most of Rex's kinfolk listened to or played and sang country music, Rex, owing to his whistling ability, began to learn to appreciate, mostly through the radio and phonograph records, early jazz songs. He especially loved Fats Waller's music, "Honeysuckle Rose" and "Ain't Misbehavin'" being two of his favorites.

"Shit, Rex," Jack once said, "you ought to move to Chicago or New York and be a famous whistler like your cousin Elmo."

"I do have a cousin named Elmo," Rex replied. "He cain't whistle a lick, though."

"Well, if you ever do, I'll be your manager. We'll travel all over the world like ol' Will Rogers and screw all the girls in Paris."

OK
'1928
Daisy

"Well, I ain't screwed any girls yet. I reckon I wouldn't even know where to start."

"You'll figure it out," said Jack. "You're only fourteen. You ain't old enough to be anybody's daddy yet."

Leonard's younger brother Elmer was Claremore's Chief of Police. Whenever he would find Rex out and about the city late in the evening, he would "arrest" him and lock him up in the police station's holding cell. Early in the morning, he would release him after giving him a modest prisoner's breakfast. Rex knew Uncle Elmer was trying to look out for him, but he also felt that he, Frank and Kilmer were probably an embarrassment to him, most of the other family members being stalwart citizens. Rex thought it was unfair that Elmer never questioned or challenged Frank or Kilmer about anything, but locked him up for nothing.

Claremore's domino parlor was owned by a Scotsman named MacVey. True to the Scot tradition, he was a thrifty businessman. Rex soon became an exceptional domino player. Perhaps it was mathematical genetics that he inherited from Leonard, but in a couple of years no one who ventured into Mac's establishment could beat him. Mac didn't allow patrons to gamble, or even buy time at the domino and pool tables with cash. First you had to purchase scrip that was only spendable at his establishment. Mac didn't want any trouble; if you had a disagreement about a wager, you could settle it any way you wanted, off the premises; in the meantime Mac had the money.

Having left the employ of the junkyard and having returned from Mexico unemployed, Rex found it difficult to sustain himself by playing dominos and shooting pool, which was the only game most of the oil field workers were willing to play him for money. An occasional trip to Tulsa usually helped his financial status, but increasingly, people were recognizing him and it was becoming more difficult to find a game of dominos.

"You ain't gonna git nowhere hangin' out with them suckers at Mac's," Frank told him, "and that Scotsman's so tight that ever'time he blinks his eyes, he skins his dick. Bootleggin' whiskey is about the only way folks like us is ever gonna git ahead," Frank explained. "I poured concrete and butchered hogs with the ol' man and all I ever got was a short dollar and a sore back."

Rex couldn't argue with Frank, but he preferred to remain independent from him. He was seventeen; Frank was twenty-one and was accustomed to calling all the shots. Morris came to Rex one day with a proposition.

"That ol' boy that married Ain't Jewell, Walter Marshall, is stashin' two five gallon tins of moonshine whiskey up in his ceiling's crawl space. I'm thinkin' we could drop by when no one's home, crawl up and grab it, and Frank said he'd give us twenty dollars for the booze."

Rex pondered Morris's proposal and upon due reflection, agreed that it could be an easy score. Hell, Walter was breaking the law himself; he and Morris removing the whiskey from his abode would put Walter in compliance. Aunt Jewell had gone to Pea Ridge, Arkansas, to visit kinfolk and what the boys knew about Walter's schedule suggested he would be gone at a certain time of day. They borrowed Frank's car and parked it in a wooded area, out of sight from the road that ran to Walter's house, and walked the remaining mile or so to the dwelling. It was easy to access the house and locate the ceiling crawl hole where the whiskey was, and after pushing the crawl space cover open with a nearby broom, Rex locked his hands together and boosted Morris up into the attic space.

"It's here, all right," Morris said. "I'll start draggin' it down to you."

Suddenly Rex heard a car pull up and footsteps coming toward the house. He was hesitant to cry out a warning to Morris for fear of Walter finding him in the large walk-in closet where the crawl space was located. It was fairly dark in the closet and Rex backed up into a row of clothes, out of sight of Walter's entrance. Morris had backed up with the first tin of whiskey and was about to turn around to hand it down to Rex when Walter, who was a tall man in his mid-fifties, jumped up and grabbed Morris's foot. Morris sensed what was happening and made sure he didn't turn to look down at Walter as Walter yelled threats and insults at whoever was the thief he had just caught and upon whose foot he was pulling.

Now Jack Burns had told Rex about a fight in Tulsa a few years earlier, where a man got knocked down, hit his head on a fire plug and never woke up. Jack had told him that there's a place on the back of the head, just above the neck, that if you hit it squarely you could render a person unconscious and if you hit it hard enough it can kill you. Well, Rex wasn't going to have Walter Marshall drag Morris out of the ceiling and then the three of them fight for the whiskey, so he measured carefully, stepped out of his hiding space, and skillfully directed a substantial blow to the base of Walter Marshall's skull. Down he went, exactly as Jack had predicted, out cold but visibly breathing.

"Shit, Morris," said Rex, "I might of just kilt ol' Walter. Grab them two tins of whiskey and let's git the hell out of here 'fore he wakes up."

Morris handed the whiskey down to Rex, scrambled down out of the attic and in a few seconds they were outside, Walter still lying face down in the closet. Walter hadn't seen the faces of either one of them and hadn't realized there were two participants.

Outside, Rex glanced inside Walter's car and seeing he had left the keys inside the ignition, decided they should haul the whiskey in Walter's car to their hidden car and leave Walter's car there. It only took a few minutes to get back to Frank's car, transfer the two tins of whiskey and drive away.

When they got back to town, they simply gave Frank back his keys and left their booty in the back seat. Frank saw their cargo and handed them a twenty dollar bill.

"Shit," Morris said, "Leonard's givin' me four bits for a day's work and we just made twenty dollars in an hour and a half. I reckon we just found a new career."

Rex didn't feel good about having cold-cocked Walter and worried that he might have killed him or injured him for life. Walter came into the domino parlor a couple of days later, no worse for wear, and did not mention the event. He wasn't friendly to Rex, as he usually was, and would not make eye contact with him. Rex, for his part, was just glad Walter was alive. Upon due reflection, despite Morris's enthusiasm, Rex decided he'd had enough of strong-armed robbery.

A few days later the town cobbler dropped by the domino parlor and challenged Rex to a game of pool. Everyone knew not to play dominos with Rex and so Rex had been forced to refine his pool-shooting to a higher level. The cobbler had played pool with Rex a few months earlier and despite losing a couple of dollars to him, had been working hard to improve his game and was now ready to challenge the domino champion to another game of pool. After the games were played and Rex had emptied the cobbler's wallet, he and Morris bought a soda and as the cobbler stood nearby, Rex began to analyze and critique the games they had just played.

"All you gotta do," said Rex, "is hit the ball where the light's shinin' on it."

"Well, you shore nuff did that," enthused Morris. "I reckon this ol' boy needs some shoes to work on 'fore he plays you ag'in."

Everyone nearby laughed. Rex continued to wax philosophical, embarrassing the thirty-five year old "sucker" in front of several people who had witnessed the game. Rex was drinking a Coca-Cola and, upon finishing the bottle's contents, was passing it back and forth from hand to hand as he sat on the edge of the pool table on which they had just played. The cobbler, with cue still in hand, leaned back quietly on a wall a few feet away and silently listened to the young brothers banter. When Rex had had his fill of celebration, he stepped forward from his seat and placed the soda bottle in the rack that was placed there for that purpose. As he stepped back and turned toward the cobbler, the cobbler swung his pool cue at Rex, hitting him across the bridge of the nose and knocking him flat on his rear end. Rex was stunned and next to helpless, but before the cobbler could kick him or swing another blow, Morris had bounced a six ball off the side of the cobbler's head and was reaching back to throw the eight ball. The cobbler dropped the cue and hastily exited, walking quickly in the opposite direction from his shoe repair shop half a block away. It took Rex a few minutes to get his bearing, at which point Morris led him once again to Doc Simpson to have his broken nose set.

"Well, hell, Rex," Doc Simpson chuckled, "if you're gonna get your damn nose broke ever'time you get in a fight with somebody, I reckon maybe you oughta try using a little diplomacy."

Rex wasn't in the mood for jokes; he was thinking about how he had waylaid Walter Marshall and how this seemed like some kind of unseen retribution. Uncle Fayette, who along with his wife had become a full-time Holiness preacher by now, had told Rex on many an occasion, "An eye for an eye" and "Ye shall reap what ye sow." He also thought about Kilmer and wondered when his wild and reckless actions might catch up with him. The next day around 9am, Rex, Morris and Frank walked to the cobbler's shoe repair shop. Unexpectedly, their Uncle Elmer was standing on the walkway in front of the business, whose door was standing wide open.

"I figured you boys would be showin' up," said Elmer. "Where's Kilmer?"

"We ain't seen 'im for a spell," Frank replied, assuming the role of spokesman for the group.

"Well, this ol' boy must have loaded his gear and headed for greener pastures during the night," Elmer said. "I run a warrant check on 'im and he's wanted in Pennsylvania for assault and battery."

"If I ever run across 'im ag'in," said Rex, "they'll be havin' a warrant out for me for assault and battery, too."

"Well, you boys can snoop around here if you want. I already looked around; there ain't nothin' left behind and don't seem like anybody knows anything about 'im, or where he might have gone. Hell, I don't think he was even here more'n a few months."

The brothers walked back to the domino parlor. Meanwhile, Rex was thinking about following Doc Simpson's advice and looking for a new line of work.

9

Miller

When Kilmer came back to town from one of his mysterious journeys, he saw Rex walking on the sidewalk across the street with his bandaged nose.

"Shit-fahr boy," he hollered across the street, "what run into you? That half-wit junkyard fella didn't come back to town, did he?"

Rex crossed the street and addressed Kilmer, "Naw, I cleaned out that cobbler fella in a game of pool and he bush-whacked me with a pool cue."

"Well, I notice his shop is emptied out and there's no sign of 'im…I knowed by lookin' in that asshole's eyes that he was trouble. I should've kicked the shit out of 'im 'fore I left town," Kilmer said.

"Naw, it weren't nothin' for you to do," Rex respond-ed. "I reckon I could've kicked the shit out of 'im, too, if I hadn't waited for that boll weevil son of a bitch to pole-axe me with a pool cue…that was plumb stupid."

"Yeah, ya gotta keep yer eyes open for trouble, son… 'specially when you're separatin' 'em from their bankroll," said Kilmer with a smile.

"Well, I'm gittin' tard of ridin' freight trains into Tulsa and Muskogee tryin' to find a domino game…shit, Kilmer, I ain't close to bein' the best pool player in these parts, but nobody can beat me at dominos and once they know who I am, I gotta play 'em pool to try to make a dollar,"

"You been ridin' a freight into Muskogee?"

"A couple of times I taken that run; there was a Negro fella over there that they said nobody could beat. I let 'im win a couple of games and we raised the stakes and I took twenty-five dollars off'n 'im. Then the other Negroes come-inse sayin' I was a domino hustler and I had to beat it out the back of the joint we was playin' at, to keep the money."

Kilmer laughed, "Boy, you kin git your damn throat cut over there in Muskogee gamblin' with them niggers… that's where ol' Harm Slade got his reputation."

"I didn't see ol' Harm over there, but them other boys looked about as mean," Rex replied.

The country brogue that most eastern Oklahomans used caused them to pronounce some "i's" with an "ah" sound. In other words, you started a "far" in the "far"place and inflated the "tars" on your automobile. Hiram was thus referred to by most locals as "Harm," rather than "Highrum." Hiram Slade was a large, rawboned black man around forty years old who, it was rumored, had killed three other black men in separate incidents with a straight razor that he carried in his back pocket for self-defense. Additionally, it was generally suspected that Hiram had been party to the killing of five white men during the 1921 Tulsa Race Riots. Those riots had been a dark day in the young state's history and after the district of Greenwood, an affluent black community, had been burned to the ground, the dust settled and not much of what had happened on either side was ever investigated. Whether or not Hiram had even been there was subject to question, but he did little to dissuade or discourage the rumors that persisted about him.

"So what're you fixin' to do?" asked Kilmer. "I reckon ol' Buster could use a hand pourin' concrete and buildin' brick walls."

"Shit, Kilmer," said Rex, "I ain't no bricklayer... hell, I could work with the ol' man, too, fer half a buck a day, if I took a notion."

"So I tell ya what, Rex, I'm gonna give you the name of a fella over at the Claremore Hotel that might be able to use you. His name is Miller...there's some ol' boys runnin' a gamblin' casino up on the top floor...shit-fahr, boy, you'd probably fit right in over there."

"I heard about that. I never went up there 'cause I figgered they'd come up with some way or 'nother to end up with whatever money a man went up there with."

"Well, think about this," said Kilmer. "If you're up there workin' for 'em, you'll be one of the ones that ends up with the money."

Kilmer and Rex laughed.

"How do I find Miller...is he Mister Miller, or is his first name Miller?" asked Rex

"It's just Miller, none of them ol' boys use first or last names and they seldom leave the floor of the hotel where they're at."

"I wonder why that is? Come to think of it, I ain't never seen any of 'em anywhere around town, even the domino parlor."

"It's ag'in' the law to run a gamblin' outfit and they sell whiskey and there's some whores up there, too."

"Shit, Kilmer," said Rex, "no wonder you're always

disappearin' for days and weeks at a time...now I know where you been goin'."

Kilmer laughed, "No Rex, I got bigger fish to fry than fleecin' these oil drillin' roughnecks and jackleg farmers. Me 'n' Miller have done some business, but not around here...a smart dog don't shit where he eats."

Kilmer looked long and hard at Rex, carefully sizing up his seventeen year old cousin. "One thing I gotta tell ya," said Kilmer, "ol' Miller's a hophead. He's prob'ly gonna want you to fetch his dope for 'im."

"I don't care one iota what he does, or who he does it with, as long as he pays me and don't try to git me to do it," said Rex.

"And look out for them whores up there," cautioned Kilmer. "You can git a case of the clap pretty easy and end up back at Doc Simpson's."

"I ain't interested in no whores, Kilmer. I got seven sisters, remember? Effie learned me to respect women and girls. Hell, me 'n' Frank run off more bird dogs and cock hounds than you could count."

"Well then, I reckon you 'n' ol' Miller might make a fit. I'll tell 'im you're comin' up to see 'im in a day or two."

Rex began to ask around town about the "casino" at the hotel. Many people knew about it, some had tried it and moved on. No one said they had ever left the premises with any winnings, although most said they witnessed other people winning. Unbeknownst to them, most of the winners were couriers for the city officials who allowed the "casino" to operate. It seemed the gamblers who ran it catered mostly to the oil field workers, local farm workers and ranch hands. In contrast to how Frank's "people" sold whiskey under the counter, up at the "casino" you could drink openly, talk and play around with whores and gamble to your heart's content. For the young men who labored in the local oil fields and nearby farmlands, it was an oasis of pleasure in a desert of

Vernon Miller

boredom and oppression.

Word got back to Rex that Miller wanted to talk with him. Rex followed the instructions of how to get to Miller's room and knocked on the door. The door opened slowly and a very large red-faced man with cold, steel-blue eyes stared out at him.

"Who're you?" the big man asked.

"I'm Rex Tanner, Kilmer's cousin,"

"Come on in," invited the man. "I'm Miller."

"Glad to know you, Miller. Kilmer says you might have some work for me."

"Kilmer says you're a domino player," Miller responded. "You any good?"

"I reckon I'm prob'ly the 'World Champion of the Midwest'," answered Rex.

"So why are you lookin' for work?"

"Nobody'll play me anymore and I ain't that good at pool…at least not good enough to know I'm always gonna win 'fore we start playin'," explained Rex.

"Well, shit, son," said Miller, "ain't that the whole secret to being successful at anything?"

"I reckon it is, come to think of it," said Rex. "What's them war ribbons over there on the dresser?"

"Aw, I was in the Army during the war and they give me them for killin' a bunch of people."

"How many people did you kill?" asked Rex uncharacteristically. "I mean, was they Germans?"

"Well, what do you think, boy? That they give me ribbons for killin' my own soldiers?"

"Naw, I mean maybe some of 'em was from other countries."

"You know it's kind of funny, when you stop to think about it," replied Miller, "but in the war you can kill as many people as you want, as long as they're on the other side. It don't matter how good of people they are, or how old, if they're men or women, or how much money they have, you just kill 'em and they give you medals. You come back home and you could kill the meanest, low-life son of a bitch God ever created and they'll fry your ass in the electric chair. They call that irony, son; you ever heard of irony?"

"Naw, I ain't never heard of it, but I git what you're a sayin'."

Rex noted that Miller hadn't answered his questions. He left it at that; even in casual conversation, Miller had an edge to him that seemed dangerous.

"So tell me, Rex, can you drive a car?"

"I reckon I'm about as good a car driver as I am a pool shooter. I'm about as good as anybody around here, but I wouldn't play some of them big city pool hustlers. I ain't got no car, though."

"Well, I got a car that I keep parked in a warehouse just outside of town. It's a Packard Phaeton. Did you ever hear of that?"

"I heard of a Packard automobile, but I never heard that other part."

"Well, it's that same car that Al Capone drives...you ever heard of Al Capone?"

"I heard of 'im. How'd you git his car?"

"Shit boy," blustered Miller, "it ain't the same car... it's the same MODEL!...and somebody else drives it for him."

"Well, whatever it is, I can drive it," replied Rex, just now noticing the Smith & Wesson .38 Special Police Revolver on the night stand next to the bed.

After seeing the handgun, Rex glanced around the room and noted a Springfield Armory 1911 .45 semi-automatic pistol on the dresser behind the ribbons that had previously caught his eye. Additionally, what appeared to be a double barreled 12 gauge shotgun was leaning up in the corner near the entrance to the bathroom.

"OK, to start with I want you to take these keys, go to the warehouse, get the car and drive to Tulsa and pick up some medicine I need. There's a doctor over there that gives me a prescription that they don't carry over here in Claremore," said Miller. "It's best to go after dark and come back before the sun comes up. If you want to do something else, park the car in a safe place, out of sight, do whatever it is first, and then pick up the medicine and come directly back to the warehouse, park the car, lock the warehouse and bring me the package and the keys. If the cops stop you, throw the package out the passenger window and try to run to the woods. If they catch you, don't say nothin'…I'll get you out if they lock you up."

"Nobody'll ever know I was there," assured Rex. "I been goin' to Tulsa on a freight train for many years now. I know big wood from brush."

"Then, as you say, I reckon you're my man," Miller said, with a smile. "Do a good job and I'll find you some other work. Here's fifty dollars and the address of the doctor. Memorize it and throw away the paper."

Miller seemed to like this brash "World Champion of the Midwest" domino player. He had noticed how Rex had scanned the room during their conversation, picking up and apparently memorizing the details of what he saw, without a break in the conversation. He was a little surprised that someone had been able to catch Rex off guard with a pool cue, but maybe that was the final exam that made him what Miller perceived him to be. Miller had known who Rex was long before Rex had ever heard of Miller. Kilmer had mentioned him several times in conversation and Miller had liked what he heard. Miller seemed to live a shadowy life, isolated from the workaday world and always on guard for the threat of intrusion. He wasn't what Rex expected a professional gambler to be, but then Rex hadn't been around any "professional" gamblers so he kept his eyes open and his mouth, for the most part, shut.

Seven Sisters

Seven sisters go out to play
Ruth and Iva and Effie Mae
Kate Juanita Louise and Pearl
They all want to dance with Leonard's girls

Work all day dance all night
Hold hands in the bright moonlight
Watch your step I heard their pa's
A razorback from Arkansas

Seven sisters grown up so tall
Every one as pretty as their old ma
You take one out for an evening walk
Her brothers are watchin' you like a hawk

Work all day dance all night
Hold hands in the bright moonlight
Better watch your step 'cause you know her pa's
A razorback from Arkansas

Seven sisters if you had one
You'd be the luckiest son of a gun
Whoever walked the sidewalks of
Rogers County where ol' Will's from

Work all day dance all night
Hold hands in the bright moonlight
Watch your step have you seen their pa
He's a razorback from Arkansas

Words & Music by Gary Rex Tanner

Rex Tanner's Sisters
Top Row: Effie Mae, Clarace, Iva, Juanita
Bottom Row: Pearl, Louise, Ruth (no photo)

10

The Oklahoma Gamblin' Man

When Rex went to the warehouse to get Miller's car, he was a bit taken aback by the automobile's stature. Rex looked several years older than his seventeen years, but he wasn't sure if his appearance matched the car and feared that he might draw suspicion from law enforcement officers.

Effie had her hands full with her young daughters, who were either teenagers or close to it by now, and her two infant sons, Charley and Bill. Leonard had never felt obligated to take responsibility for training any of the children, except for Frank, and Rex did what he could to give her money and police his younger sisters. Rex thought it would be a good idea to take one of his sisters when he went to Tulsa. Perhaps the appearance of a wealthy young man out driving with his girlfriend in a fancy car would draw less suspicion than him going alone. The girls were eager to accompany him and ride in Miller's Packard.

Rex would go early in the afternoon, park the car in a secure location and take whichever sister it was to a moving picture show. Movies had sound by now and Tulsa had a nice theater. After the movie, he would take his sister out for a nice dinner and then visit the doctor for Miller's "medicine." Rex knew that he was picking up heroin for Miller, but he had been told that doctors could "prescribe" the drug for some patients and so he wasn't too worried about being caught. Besides, Rex and his sisters walking around town, going to the movies and having dinner didn't rouse much attention. Miller had a mechanic that regularly visited the warehouse and serviced the Packard, so Rex didn't even have to stop for gas. The fifty dollars Miller gave him each time paid for all the expenses, including the "prescription", and Rex still had twenty-five dollars left over. That was much better than boarding a freight train to Muskogee, riding with a bunch of hobos and taking a chance on getting your throat cut. He went to Tulsa in the Packard once a week, and Miller slowly began giving him other chores to do for him. Rex liked the money and driving the Packard. Eventually, Miller would have Rex bring him pastries and other food items, several days a week, early in the mornings.

As Miller became more comfortable with his young charge, he taught him the process of how to prepare his heroin shots. Sometimes, when Miller was especially shaky, Rex would make the injection.

After a couple of months, Miller advised Rex that he would be leaving town for a short time. No details about where or when he might be back were offered, but Miller told Rex to go over to the gambling rooms and talk to "Bernie." He told him that Bernie would give him some work while he was gone, and Miller gave Rex a hundred dollars to sustain himself while he was away. Rex had a room at the hotel by now that Miller paid for, and he had met Bernie a couple of times in passing. In a couple of days Miller was gone. Rex went by the warehouse out of curiosity and found the Packard gone, too. Rex found Bernie and related what Miller had told him.

"I guess I can use you," said Bernie. "Miller says you're a good kid and your uncle's the God damn Chief of Police."

Rex wasn't sure if Bernie meant being Elmer's nephew was a plus or a minus.

"So Miller says you're already a gambler."

"Naw, not like you're talkin' about," said Rex. "I'm a domino player, but the way I play it ain't gamblin'."

Bernie laughed out loud. "You ever play blackjack or roll dice?"

"I played enough to know how to play, but I ain't never played enough to win any real money, like dominos."

"Well, son, we're kind of like you and dominos: we ain't really gamblin' either, 'cause we already know we're gonna win, so here's how we'll start. I'll show you how to deal seconds, which means you figure out what the top card in the deck is by flashing it to a whore, or another 'plant' of some kind. They'll give you a signal and if it helps the player you're givin' it to's hand, you slide the next card out and give it to him."

"So how do you know what the second card is?" asked Rex.

"It don't matter, you already increased your odds by taking away the good card he was going to get. He may still win the hand, but over a period of time, the odds will take their toll and he'll lose whatever money he decides to bet. Shit, Rex, the dealer already has the odds in his favor; you don't have to cheat them on every hand. Just once in a while and you'll always come out on top," explained Bernie. "So here, I'll show you the technique of dealing seconds and you practice until you think you've got it. In the meantime, you can be a shill and we'll teach you how to signal the dealer when he flashes that top card to you."

"So I'll be like one of the whores?" Rex said wryly.

"Yeah, like that," Bernie said, laughing. "Don't worry, you'll be dealin' relief in a couple of weeks."

Bernie wasn't as generous as Miller, but the money was still good and Rex was learning a new trade. Rex didn't see much difference in taking other gamblers' money in this new way and taking it in a domino game. Either way, they weren't going to win.

Bernie had neglected to explain the other advantages the house had at the blackjack table. While the whores did occasionally accompany a customer to a private room, their main function was to distract the men who were gambling and encourage them to drink more whiskey. A drunk with a whore hanging on him is an easy mark and after he's been cleaned out, he has no money left to pay the whore.

The dice table was a bit more difficult to manipulate. The whores still served the same function, but the dice were a bit more unpredictable. Bernie's crew used the same type of techniques, switching dice and other less effective practices. Their main advantage, besides the odds always being in their favor, was a young hustler from New Jersey named "Quick Johnny Slick." Quick Johnny had hands like a concert pianist, with the touch of a safe cracker, and had learned to "coax" the dice into coming up with the number he wanted more than seventy-five percent of the time. For practice he would spend hours rolling the dice from double aces to double sixes and back again. As a rule, Bernie wouldn't have Johnny roll a bunch of sevens and elevens. That would seem too obvious. First he would roll a double number, usually a four or a ten and then depending on how the bets were placed, roll a seven or the point he needed. Johnny didn't stay at the table too long, so no one knew he was part of the syndicate. He generally came in when the croupier was having trouble using the usual methods. Rex was amazed at Johnny's skill. He would watch him practice and still it was hard to believe he was doing it with standard dice. Since Rex had an affinity for numbers, he was often the shill, keeping track of which number was to the house's advantage for Johnny Slick to roll and making the undetected signal.

One evening Rex stopped by at the local coffee shop after his shift. It was near closing time and he found a table near the rear of the dining area. Two roughnecks from the oil fields, in their mid to late twenties, came in while Rex was having his meal. They sat at the counter and looked around. Seeing Rex, they recognized him as the blackjack dealer that had just separated them from a month's pay. They were large, tough-looking men, obviously in a foul mood.

"Hey card shark!" yelled one of the roughnecks. "Where's your girlfriend?"

"You mean that whore you was kissin' while you was throwin' away your money?" returned Rex.

"No, I mean your Mama," shot back the other roughneck.

Rex sipped his drink slowly, sizing up the two men, trying to decide the best way to handle the situation.

"You think you're pretty God damned smart, cheatin' us out of a month's pay. Now you're down here eatin' dinner on us and here we are thinkin' maybe you oughta give us our money back," said the first roughneck.

"Naw, we don't give nothin' back," said Rex, "but come on back next month and maybe you'll have better luck."

Infuriated, the roughneck doing most of the talking said, "Tell you what, boy, you ain't leavin' here in one piece unless we get back our money that you cheated us out of."

"Well, then I reckon we'll have a go. Let's see…two of you big ol' ignert shit kickers and one of me…that's about even odds…"

Suddenly the front door of the café opened and in walked Frank and Kilmer.

"Hey cousin," Kilmer said, glancing at Rex.

Before Frank and Kilmer had removed their coats and seated themselves, the two roughnecks grabbed whatever they were carrying and quickly darted out the door. "What the hell's wrong with them?" asked Kilmer.

"Maybe they left their bulldog tied up outside and when they saw you come in, they run out to go check on it," Rex said, laughing.

Kilmer and Frank joined in the laughter. The three ate their meals, and Rex never encountered the two roughnecks again.

11

The Arkansas Traveler

Rex usually worked in the casino during the evenings, which left his mornings and afternoons free. He was a sharp dresser and was especially particular about the appearance of his shoes. His pal Lex Lockhart, a young black man, had a shoeshine stand near the domino parlor that Rex regularly frequented. Whenever Rex would pass by between shoe shines, Lex would invite him to jump up in an empty chair if one was available and Lex would give his shoes a quick touch up at no charge. One day while Rex was sitting in one of the elevated chairs at the shoeshine stand shooting the breeze with Lex, a large square jawed gentleman in what appeared to be an expensive ill fitting double breasted suit walked up. Lex invited him to take the empty chair next to Rex.

"How much for a shine?" the big man asked.

"Two bits" answered Lex, more than doubling the

price he charged locals.

"All right then, take after it."

The big man awkwardly climbed up into the empty chair and Lex began cleaning the man's leather shoes in preparation for the shoe shine he was about to administer. Rex and the gentleman hadn't acknowledged each other to this point and Rex opened with:

"That's a smart lookin' suit of clothes you got there mister."

"Thank you son," said the man who looked to be around thirty years old.

"My name's Rex and this gentleman shinin' your shoes is Lex."

"Rex and Lex, you boys ain't cousins air ya?"

"Naw," replied Lex before Rex could answer, "We's brothers…a course Ise the black sheep of the fambly."

"Shit boys, that's right God damn funny. Say Lex, one of them new shoes I bought don't shine quite as bright as the other one. See if you can even 'em up a little."

"Sho nuff mistuh, ever'one know that lef shoe always shine better den dat right shoe."

"I always wondered about that," the man said. "By the way my name's Bradley."

Rex had remained silent after Bradley had insulted the two friends; studying him and sizing him up. Lex had skillfully turned what could have been an uncomfortable situation into a light and friendly mood.

"So where y'all from, Bradley?" inquired Rex.

"Ahm from Hoxie Arkansas."

"So what y'all doin' around these parts?" asked Rex.

"Wail, I tell ya Ray-ex, my mama took up with this ol' boy in Hoxie when I uz about tin year old. She died and that mean ol' son of a bitch raised me. He had two sons older'n me and two daughters younger'n me. After mama died, the ol' man and his sons worked me like a mule for fifteen years, feedin' me on the worst God damn vittles you could imagine. Still, I growed big and strong like I am now and when he caught me takin' liberties with his new young wife and his two daughters, him and his two boys come to whoop my ass. I reckon they didn't bring all the help they needed and I almost kilt one of the sons, broke the other one's laig and maybe blinded the ol' man. I knowed I uz in a jackpot and I lit out for Little Rock like a scalded dog for fear of gittin' hung by the local sheriff, who was a friend of the ol' man. There's more to the story but I ain't gonna git into it right now. Say, you don't know where a man kin git a drink a whiskey, do ya?"

"Reckon I do," replied Rex.

"Wail, here's a five dollar bill. Why'n't y'all go git me a pint and I'll share it with you boys and you can keep the change."

"Awright Bradley, I'll be back in half an hour."

Rex took the five dollars, went to the taxi stand and bought a pint of whiskey from Frank for two dollars. When he returned, Lex and Bradley were waiting for him with three paper cups they had secured from inside the domino parlor.

"Here boys, I'll pour," said Bradley taking the bottle from Rex and pointing it toward Lex's cup and then Rex's. "So Ray-ex, I hears they's a high stakes card game here in Claremore. Y'all knows how to git a man a drink a whiskey, I wonder does ya'll know anything about gittin' in a card game?"

"I tell you what Bradley, I do know somethin' about that. Maybe after we drink this pint we can see what I can conjure up."

Bradley drank his whiskey quickly as Lex and Rex barely sipped theirs. When Bradley turned away Rex poured his in the gutter behind his back and accepted another pour. Lex begged off another drink saying he had to work the rest of the day and that his customers wouldn't appreciate him having whiskey on his breath. A half-hour later the bottle was empty and Bradley sent Rex with another five dollar bill to fetch another pint. It was mid-afternoon when Rex suggested they could rent a hotel room and set up a card game. Bradley was eager to get started and Rex took him over to the hotel where he worked and had Bradley rent a room on a lower floor; never mentioning the casino upstairs. While Bradley was being shown his room, Rex hurried up to the casino, got a rack of chips from the storage cabinet and told Bernie he wouldn't be in later that night.

"Looks to me like you got a live one on the string Rex," said Bernie.

"Reckon maybe I do, I'll know in a couple of hours."

"Just watch your ass boy, don't do nothin' stupid."

Rex hurriedly left for the domino parlor and found three acquaintances to occupy the other places at the table. He told them that they could bet whatever they had, which wasn't much, and that if they lost he would reimburse them their losses. The four men came back to Bradley's room with another pint of whiskey and the game began. The five men agreed that the game would be blackjack and since Rex was the bank, he was given the deal. Everyone bought whatever denominations of chips they wanted. The three acquaintances each bought ten fifty-cent chips and five one dollar chips. Bradley said he wanted to play for a hundred dollars a hand so Rex gave him ten hundred dollar chips for a thousand dollars. Of course Rex hadn't put anything in the "bank" so if Bradley won, there was no money to cover his chips and Rex knew that he could end up like the old man and his two sons that Bradley had told him about earlier in the day. On the other hand, Rex knew Bradley was never going to win, hell he was too drunk and too dumb to realize that Rex was playing without putting up any money. After an hour, Bradley bought another thousand dollars worth of chips. At 10pm he was down twenty-six hundred dollars. The three gentlemen who had joined Rex and Bradley had each won ten or twelve dollars and said they had to go. Bradley's roll of bills that he carried in his front pocket looked to be about half its original size. Bradley was philosophical about his losses. Drinking the last of the whiskey, which Rex hadn't touched since the first drink earlier in the day, he began to complete the story he had previously begun to tell Lex and Rex at the shoe shine stand.

"So I uz hitchin' 'long the side of the road on the way to Little Rock when I comes upon this great big semi truck full of chickens. The two boys that was drivin' was stopped by the side of the road takin' a piss and I asked 'em iffen I could flag a ride. They was right rude and they laughed and said they warn't ridin' along with no back woods goober like me. I thought about it fer a minute and then just decided to kick the shit out of 'em and take their truck. I worked 'em over pretty good, they was bloody and cryin' and pukin' and crawlin' around tryin' to find someplace to hide from me when I drove off. Shit Ray-ex, I couldn't hardly drive that rig, but somehow I got to Little Rock and son of a bitch, first thing out of the box a couple of ol' boys come up and asked me what I'd take for the truck. To make that long story short, I sold 'em the truck, trailer and the whole load of chickens and all the cages for six thousand bucks. That's where I got the money to play cards and buy this here suit. Shit-fahr Ray-ex, I never had no money before; all my life I just worked like a slave and got treated like a dog. Ray-ex, how 'bout you sleep here tonight and we'll git 'er goin' ag'in in the mornin'. I'd like a chance to win my money back; maybe this time I won't drink so much whiskey."

Rex immediately remembered the bunkhouse incident with the half-wit. Bradley was a much more formidable threat and Morris wouldn't be around to help him if indeed trouble did occur.

"Tell ya what Bradley, I got to go see my mama and

check on my sisters. I'll meet y'all at the coffee shop down the street from the domino parlor and we'll git 'er goin' ag'in tomorra."

"Awright Ray-ex, about ten in the mornin'?"

"Yeah, that's a good time, I'll see you then."

Rex casually boxed up the chips and deposited the twenty-six hundred dollars he had won and rolled up in his front pocket, the same as Bradley had done and Miller always did. He took his time, never turning his back or taking his eye off Bradley. He calmly opened the door, entered the hallway and walked downstairs and out into the night.

The next morning Rex went to the coffee shop where he was to meet Bradley and ordered breakfast. Bradley didn't appear and Rex finished his breakfast, ordered another cup of coffee and waited. Presently, through the coffee shop door entered his uncle Elmer. Elmer made his way to where Rex was sitting at the counter and confronted him directly.

"Do you know an ol' boy name of Bradley Hankins?"

"Naw, I don't reckon I do," answered Rex.

"Well some folks are sayin' they seen you with 'im yesterday and that you rented a hotel room with 'im."

"Aw shit Elmer, I know who you mean now. I never rented nuthin' with 'im…he said he didn't have no place to stay and I showed 'im where the hotel was. I spent the night out at Effie's."

"Well he's a fugitive from justice and he robbed some folks over in Arkansas and hurt 'em real bad. Sold a chicken truck for six thousand dollars, too. We caught up with 'im this mornin' and he's over at the police station in a cell. Looks like he's about three thousand dollars short of what he stole…you know anything about that?"

"Three thousand dollars? Are you shittin' me?"

"Rex, if you have any of that money you could be an accomplice."

"Uncle Elmer, if I had any of that money I wouldn't

be sittin' here talkin' to you."

"You're pretty clever Rex, I don't think a man would be able to figure out whether you had it or not. Tell you what though, we're gonna be keepin' an eye on you. If you got it, you ain't gonna be able to spend it."

With that Elmer finished the cup of coffee he had been drinking, walked to the door and departed the coffee shop. Rex never heard anything more about his friend from Hoxie, Arkansas. It was true he wasn't able to spend the money without drawing attention from Elmer and his officers. No one was watching Effie though and for the next couple of years her burden was eased considerably.

12

Don't Take Me Back To Tulsa

Miller returned a few weeks later, stayed a month and then departed again with the rest of the gambling crew and whores. Only Rex and Johnny Slick stayed behind. Miller told Rex that some of the local citizenry were complaining about their operation and that they were leaving to let things cool down for a while. Miller added that they might be setting up another gambling casino, perhaps in Kansas or even Canada. Miller and Bernie knew Rex wasn't interested in moving to another locale. They told Johnny Slick that they would let him know when they got the new operation up, so he could join them. It was a bit of a loose group. Sometimes one of the syndicate members would leave and another take his place. Usually, though, there were always five or six members, not including Rex or Johnny. The whores were a bit more consistent, but they too would sometimes leave and be replaced by someone else.

Although Rex appeared older than his years, the whores liked to try to embarrass him by teasing him with sexual innuendo. Rex was good-natured about it, but it was clear he wanted no part of whatever they were selling or giving away. Eventually, they left him alone and simply referred to him as "Sexy Rexy."

Even though they had money, Rex and Johnny didn't have much to do to occupy themselves while they waited for Miller and/or the gamblers to return.

"Jack Burns told me about a crap game over in Tulsa where we could probably make some dough," Rex said to Johnny.

"Well hell, Rex, we know how it all works, we oughta be able to take it from the house just as easy as takin' it from the suckers."

Rex and Johnny rode the freight train to Tulsa, found the game that Jack Burns had mentioned and began to play. Quick Johnny rolled the dice; Rex read the field and placed bets. In half an hour they had over eight hundred dollars, including the hundred dollars they had brought with them. The man overseeing the game stopped the game and called for a half hour intermission to re-fund the house because of the heavy losses. While Rex and Johnny were standing around, a dapper forty-something year old man approached them.

"Boys," he said, "I been seein' what you're doin' here and I want to tell you, you're playin' for peanuts stickin' around here. There's a big game just outside of town, where some of the big oil company executives and other local rich folks play. I'd want a reasonable percentage, but I could take you out there and get you in the game…I'm not talkin' hundreds of dollars…I'm talkin' thousands."

"That sounds like what we're lookin' for," said Johnny Slick. "How much of a percentage are you talkin' about?"

"Well, I think twenty-five percent would be fair,"

said the gentleman.

"How 'bout twenty," said Johnny. "Hell, me 'n' Rex have to split whatever we win between us…you'd get twenty and we'd each get forty."

"Hell, boys, I ain't gonna argue with you about it… twenty percent of somethin' is better than twenty-five percent of nothin'."

"All right, then," said Rex, "let's blow this dump and go find the high rollers."

The gentleman led them to his Buick automobile and they drove away from the building where they had won the money.

"So what's your names, boys? I'm Fred."

"I'm Rex and this is Johnny Slick."

"Johnny Slick?" laughed Fred. "How'd you get named that? You had to of made that up."

"No, not exactly," said Johnny. "Our family name is Van Slyke. People read it and think I'm Van Slike, or Van Slick. I just dropped the Van and pronounced it the way most people around here do and it comes out 'Johnny Slick'. I got fast hands so people started callin' me 'Quick Johnny Slick'."

"That's a good story," said Fred. "The way you roll those dice, I'm sure I'll be hearin' more about you."

The car was at the outskirts of town by now and Fred headed out a lightly traveled country road to make their destination.

About five miles out of town Fred said, "There it is! Look, you can't even see any light comin' out."

"It's sure as hell dark," said Rex. "How come there's no cars around?"

"Most of 'em are parked in the barn and some are out there behind the barn. They've made a parkin' lot out there where you can't see 'em from the road."

"That's smart," said Johnny. "Rich folks always

think ahead like that."

Fred drove up near the old farmhouse and pointed out where the players were and stopped the car and killed the ignition. "Let's go make some money," he said, and they all exited the vehicle.

A few steps from the car, Fred said, "Wait a minute, I think I left the keys in the ignition."

He re-entered the car and suddenly the car started and the headlights went on. Rex and Johnny were standing several steps in front of the car as Fred came out the driver's side with a .38 Smith & Wesson revolver and said, "All right, you shit-heels, start emptyin' your pockets…and I mean ALL the money."

Rex and Johnny were stunned. Their dreams of taking a group of rich folks to the cleaners had suddenly become a nightmare. Not only that, but now they were out their eight hundred dollars, which included their one hundred dollars seed money.

"Roll that money up in a wad and put it on the hood of the car," instructed Fred, "and don't even think of challenging me…you wouldn't be the first penny ante hustlers I buried out in the woods."

Rex and Johnny weren't thinking anything, other than how stupid they were and how easily Fred had conned them.

"So here it is boys. We don't cotton to no out of towners comin' in here and hustlin' our game. You boys are pretty good, I'll admit, but I seen what you was up to five minutes after you got in the game. I don't know where you're from, or who you know, but don't ever come back around here again…do you understand me?"

Rex and Johnny both nodded in the affirmative.

"Are you gonna take our shoes?" asked Rex.

"Your shoes?" laughed Fred. "Why would I want your shoes?"

"Well," said Rex, "the last time someone throwed a gun on me and took my money, they made me give 'em my shoes."

"Shit Rex, if I ever see you again, you ain't gonna need no shoes."

With Fred still pointing the revolver at them, he scooped the money from the hood of the car, slid under the steering wheel of the Buick, turned around and drove out the long driveway that led to the abandoned farm house. The night was pitch black. Rex and Johnny slowly slogged their way back to town and then waited along the railroad tracks for the afternoon freight back to Claremore.

Charles "Pretty Boy" Floyd

13

Pretty Boy Floyd

Miller and the gamblers eventually returned to Claremore and resumed their "casino" operation. Rex served as Miller's personal aide and worked at the blackjack tables and dice game with Quick Johnny when he was idle. Miller paid him well, as did the gamblers by now, and he made sure Effie and his sisters had what they needed. One night Rex heard a loud banging at his hotel room door. Opening the door, he was brushed back into the room by his brother Frank.

"I got Floyd downstairs in a taxi," said Frank. "Elmer and his cops are all gone home and the FBI is out all over the place lookin' for 'im. They got a description of the clothes he's wearin' and you're about his size. What you got that we can give 'im?"

"Floyd?" Rex asked. "You mean Floyd the bank robber?"

"Yeah, Floyd the bank robber, Charles Floyd."

"So are you quittin' bootleggin' and gonna rob banks now?"

"I ain't robbed no banks yet and I ain't got a lotta time to waste, just tell me what ya got."

In contrast to his usually calm demeanor, Frank seemed uncharacteristically animated. He began to scan the room for anything that might be of use to him.

"Shit, Frank, alls I got is that cashmere sweater I just paid twenty dollars for…"

"Yeah, that's good, nobody'll be looking for Floyd wearin' a cashmere sweater…what the hell's a cashmere, anyway?"

"I reckon it's some kind of special wool, or somethin'. It's pretty soft…I reckon I got some wool slacks, too… shit, Frank, I was plannin' on wearin' that shit myself. I ain't even wore any of it yet."

Frank hardly heard anything that Rex said beyond what related to his task at hand. Frank naturally had an executive mind and was wholly focused on what he had committed himself to do.

"Just give it to me; better give me that new pair of shoes you got in that box over there, too."

"You mean they got a description out on his shoes?"

"Hell, I don't know, but if I'm gonna git 'im over to Muskogee tonight, he's gonna look good for whoever's waitin' for 'im."

"You're goin' to Muskogee?"

"Yeah, there's some folks out in the country that have a farm he can stay at 'til the heat's off."

Rex reluctantly gave Frank his clothing items, and Frank was out the door and into the night. As an older brother, Frank had lost his influence over Rex at an early age. This night, however, Frank was in complete control and Rex comfortably and naturally assumed the role of subordinate to his older brother.

The next day Frank returned to Rex's hotel room with a bundle of clothes and a pair of expensive imported leather shoes.

"Floyd says thanks for the clothes. Hell, we didn't even see anyone after we left here," said Frank.

"Shit, Frank, this looks like a hundred dollar suit... and these shoes probably cost more than that."

"There's a fifty dollar bill in one of them jacket pockets, too. Floyd says you can use that to git everything dry-cleaned."

"How'd you run into Floyd?" inquired Rex.

"Miller set it up. We got a phone call at the taxi stand that someone of 'prominence' needed a lift out to Muskogee, so I took a cab and went myself. Shit, I thought it was gonna be Will Rogers. When I got to the address, out walked Floyd and away we went."

"Miller knows Floyd?"

"Well, shit, Rex, I didn't git into it with 'im, but he must know 'im if he orders a cab for 'im."

"So what'd you talk to Floyd about on the way over to Muskogee? You try 'n' sell 'im some whiskey?"

"Whiskey, my ass. We was both cranin' our necks lookin' for any sign of the FBI...we didn't have time for whiskey OR talkin'."

"So what did you charge 'im?"

"Didn't charge 'im nothin'. Shit, Rex, he's a bank robber, for Christ's sake. I just kept my mouth shut and when we got to his hideout, he give me two hundred dollars and told me to give you this suit of clothes with that fifty dollar bill in the pocket."

Rex followed Floyd's instructions and had all the clothes dry-cleaned. The suit was a little big, but Rex delighted in wearing it at the blackjack table while he flirted with the whores and fleeced the clientele. Something about

Floyd's suit gave Rex a bit of a feeling of recklessness. No one knew how Rex had come into possession of such impressive haberdashery items, and Rex was not about to tell anyone. It was two-plus years into the Great Depression and not too many men walked around Claremore, Oklahoma in a hundred dollar suit and imported leather shoes.

A couple of years later Frank would join the crowd of people that attended Floyd's funeral, by far the most ever in the state of Oklahoma.

J

14

Wanted In Wichita

Bernie the gambling boss took Rex aside one day and asked him, "Hey Rex, we're goin' on a little trip in a couple of weeks and we need someone to do some drivin'. Maybe you'd like to come along and help us out?"

"I don't know, Bernie," Rex replied. "Where would we be goin'?"

"We can talk about that later; by the way, Miller's the one that suggested I ask you."

In a few hours Rex found Kilmer and related to him what Bernie had said. Kilmer was negative to the idea, saying, "It's OK to hang around those people as long as you're around here and you have me 'n' Elmer and your brothers and even your pa, iffen you need us. I been on some of them 'trips' with them fellas, and they're a different bunch out there on the road…it's not somethin' you want to git involved in."

"Yeah, OK," said Rex.

Rex was curious about what Bernie was referring to as a "trip". Still, he knew from the beginning of his association with Miller, Bernie and their associates, not to question anything that had to do with anything outside the casino.

"Hey, I heard you went and got religion," said Rex.

"Yeah, my Daddy brought me to this ol' preacher boy that's got a tent revival and after I talked to 'im for about an hour, I decided to join his flock and go out on the road out to California with 'im."

"Well, you don't reckon that's what Miller and Bernie are fixin' to do, too, do ya Kilmer?" joked Rex

"Naw," Kilmer replied, "I reckon it's better you don't know what Miller and Bernie do when they leave Claremore."

"Aw, I uz just actin' a fool. So I'm thinkin' your daddy was pretty glad to hear you was takin' up with a preacher, him being a preacher himself and all…and your mama, too."

"Well, I reckon that's true. I think the preacher's puttin' me in charge of takin' up the collection."

Rex laughed out loud. Kilmer hesitated for a moment and then joined him, realizing what he had just said.

"Kilmer, that preacher's smarter'n a fox…hell, anyone seein' you passin' that basket around is gonna think hard about tryin' to hold anything back. Hell, you'll probably git all their watches and jewelry, too."

"Well, it's all for the Lord now, Rex…I reckon He'll know what to do with jewelry and watches; if not, I'll take care of it for Him."

"When are you headin' for California?" asked Rex.

"In a couple of weeks…that's what the preacher says."

Rex talked to Bernie a day or two later and declined his offer. He didn't mention that he'd talked to Kilmer; he just said he needed to stay close to town so he could help

Effie with his sisters. Everyone, including Bernie, knew that Effie had a tough row to hoe with Leonard, whose alcoholic irresponsibility was continuing to cause problems within the family.

Rex spoke with Quick Johnny Slick and found out that he wasn't going on the "trip" either; in fact, he hadn't been asked. A couple of days later Rex saw Johnny Slick at the café where they usually had their meals. Spring was turning to summer in nineteen-thirty-three and it was getting harder and harder for a man to find a way to keep his head above water.

"So Rex," began Johnny, "whatta you think we oughta do to make a buck? We can't go back to Tulsa and there ain't nothin' for us around here."

"My ol' buddy Jack Burns says they're hirin' workers over at the wheat fields in Lyons, Kansas. I might take a notion to go over there, but I don't reckon it would be anything you'd be interested in," answered Rex.

"Well, they probably wouldn't rob us after they paid us," said Johnny. "I might give it a go…if you went, too."

"Well, shit-fahr, Johnny Slick, let's figure out the train schedule and hit the road."

The two men asked around about where the northbound freight went and were told they could catch a freight that went north through Wichita, Kansas, and then stopped in Lyons, Kansas, where it was easy to disembark. Rex and Johnny bundled some extra clothes and food together and stealthily boarded the freight just north of Claremore. There were several hobos and obviously out of work men, probably doing the same thing they were…going around the country looking for any work they could find. When the train came into the greater Wichita area, Rex and Johnny were surprised to see most of the free-riders bailing off the train before it came into the station area.

"I wonder what's wrong with them ol' boys?" said

Rex.

"They're probably just goin' to Wichita and want to get off someplace where no one can see 'em," speculated Johnny.

"Yeah, we'll just duck back here behind the door and no one will ever know we was here," said Rex.

The train stopped, and a few minutes later a man in a blue uniform and waving a baton jumped into the boxcar with them and instructed them to exit the boxcar. They were herded to another area where a small group of men who had failed to depart the train as it came into Wichita were standing and being guarded by another couple of "Railroad Bulls" and a Sheriff.

"Come on, boys," said the Sheriff, "we're goin' to see the judge."

The men were marched a mile or so to the courthouse. The judge was called and came down to the sidewalk and sentenced the half-dozen or so men to thirty days of hard labor for vagrancy and riding a public utility vehicle without permission. The men were marched another few blocks to the city jail, where they were instructed that they had a choice of working a twelve hour shift every day, in which case they would be given two meals each day, or remaining in their cell for the duration of their sentence and being given bread and water. They were given the remainder of the day to make their decision.

"I ain't afraid of hard work," said Rex to Johnny. "Sittin' here in a cell for thirty days on bread and water is gonna make the time go by twice as slow."

"Shit, Rex, I ain't workin' for these assholes. I'll eat bread and water for a month. They can kiss my ass. I've been in worse jackpots than this."

"Well, I'm gonna go give it a try and see what happens."

The two men gave the overseer their decisions, and

the next day Rex was loaded onto a large truck with a couple of dozen other men and sent out to do road maintenance.

"What are you in here for?" asked one of the older men in the group.

"Aw, we uz takin' a freight over to Lyons, Kansas, and when we stopped in Wichita, the Railroad Bulls got us," replied Rex.

"Yeah," the man said, "they keep this truck full with people that make the mistake of not jumping off the train as it comes into town and then walking around the town and hopping the train again as it leaves Wichita. What'd they give you…thirty days?"

"Yeah," said Rex, "on this road gang, or with bread and water in a cell."

"See that ol' boy over there in the back of the truck with the red bandana?" said the man.

"Yeah."

"Well, they give him thirty days over two years ago and he's still here…most of us have been on this gang well over the thirty days they give us."

"Shit! You mean they don't let you out when your time's done?"

"Naw, they find somethin' you done wrong to extend your sentence and keep you here workin' on the road crews. Some guys don't care 'cause there ain't no work, anyway… they figure at least they're eatin' a couple of times a day."

"Well, they ain't gonna extend me. I'm gonna toe the line and git out of here in thirty days."

"You'll see," said the man, adding, "and if you try to run, they'll catch you with them dogs you see in that truck behind us, and that's how they keep you here."

Rex was nonplussed after hearing how things worked on the Wichita road gang. He began to study the terrain and noticed a two-lane highway off in the distance as the truck began to climb the hill to where the day's work was to be done. Rex surveyed the surrounding area in his mind and estimated the distance to the road to be about three to four hundred yards beyond a thicket of trees, which lay in the direction the road gang was heading. When the crews were dispatched, Rex studied where the trucks were parked and how the dogs were tied, as well as the protocol for being given water and breaks for the prisoners to relieve themselves. The prisoners were first told to urinate before the work day began, so that no one could take advantage and leave the work area. They were told to take their bowel movements back at the jail and that if they failed to do so and had to do it in the field, they would forfeit their evening meal. Rex kept eyeing that thicket, which now lay about a hundred yards from where they were working, between them and the highway another couple of hundred yards or so below. He decided that if they came back to the same area the next day, he was going to try to figure out a way to get to the thicket and then attempt to get to the highway. What he was going to do once he made the highway was unclear in his mind, but he had always managed to think quickly in a crisis, and he hoped something would occur to expedite his escape. Later that night, back at the jail he talked with Johnny Slick.

"It ain't that bad, Johnny; the food's all right and I've had to work harder."

"I'm telling you, Rex, I ain't goin'. I only got 29 days to go…the bread's stale and the water tastes like horse piss, but I'd rather sit here flat on my ass than to work for them bastards."

"Well, iffen I don't see you anymore, I reckon it's been good to know you," said Rex.

"Where you think you're goin'? You thinkin' of runnin'?"

"Naw, they say if you run and they catch you--and they say they always do, 'cause of the dogs--they just tack on more time."

"That's why I'm takin' the bread and water, Rex, I heard about how these jerkwater towns get free labor by gettin' you in jail and then trumpin' up shit to tack on to your sentence."

"Yeah, an ol' boy was sayin' that this morning on the way to the place we was workin' today. I sure ain't gonna fall into that trap."

Rex didn't see any point in telling Johnny of his plans. Since Johnny had elected to do the time in his cell, he would be of no use to Rex and if he didn't have any information to trade the guards for something, like food, he couldn't hurt him.

The next day, as Rex had hoped, the crew returned to the same area where they had been the day before. As they worked and came slightly closer to the thicket, Rex called out, "Cap'n! I need to take a shit."

"You're supposed to shit at the jail," replied the guard.

"I tried, but nothin' came out. I reckon I'm gonna shit my pants in a minute or two."

"It's gonna cost you your evenin' meal, I reckon you know that."

"It don't matter about that right now, sir, 'cause I got to shit bad, and that's all I'm thinkin' about."

"All right then," said the guard, "see that thicket over yonder? You got five minutes to get over there and shit and five more to get your ass back over here and get back to work. Any of the rest of you son of a bitches that want to give up dinner can go over there with him."

Rex was glad there were no takers and put down his shovel and began walking to the thicket.

The guard called out, "Don't forget I got these here dogs, and if you run they'll catch you and eat your God damn balls."

Rex stopped just before he entered the thicket and

Daisy

waved back to the guard that he was going in. As soon as he disappeared from sight he ran through the thicket and out the other side and down the hill to the highway. He was a fast runner and sure-footed, but he fell a couple of times and rolled, getting up and continuing to run without breaking stride. Out of breath, he reached the road just as a large truck hauling hay was approaching him. Rex stepped out into the road and waved his arms and the gentleman driving the truck slowed down and stopped.

"Get in son," the driver invited.

Rex was in the truck in an instant. Out of breath and dirty from falling, he made a curious sight for the driver who, thankfully for Rex, had resumed speed and was putting distance between him and the road gang.

"What happened to you, boy?" the man asked.

"I uz hitchin' a ride with these two assholes and they pulled off the side of the road and robbed me. I kicked the shit out of one of 'em, but the other one got my roll, and they left me on the side of the road and you come around the bend just as they went out of sight," explained Rex.

"Well, that's a hell of a note," sympathized the driver. "Where are you headed?"

"I reckon 'bout as far as you can take me."

"Well, I'm takin' this load of hay over to Lyons to some folks for their livestock,"

"Lyons is all right with me," said Rex, trying not to show a reaction to his sudden good fortune.

"So where you headed after that?" further questioned the driver.

"Well, times is pretty tough. I'm mostly lookin' for someplace to work for a while 'til I can git my bankroll back up where I can survive."

"I tell you what, I knows them people where I'm takin' this hay pretty well. They're most always lookin' for a good hand this time of year...maybe you can do some work for them…I think they got a bunkhouse where you could sleep, and the wife's always feedin' me when I come by… maybe they'll throw in meals if you work cheap enough."

"Shit, Mister, I ain't in no position to be askin' for much. I'd pretty much take whatever they uz offerin'."

In a couple of hours they were at the farm where the hay was to be delivered. The driver introduced Rex to the farmer and his wife and explained Rex's plight.

"Well, that's a God damn shame son, them two bastards robbin' you and all. We got lots of wheat to harvest in a couple of weeks," said the farmer. "Today's the 4th of July, you know, so we're not workin' the rest of the weekend."

Suddenly Rex realized that his "great escape" had come on his twentieth birthday. Independence Day! *Now that's irony, as Miller might say*, thought Rex.

"Tell you what, son," the farmer continued, "I'll pay you two dollars a day, which is usually around ten hours, and Julie here will feed you three meals a day, and you can sleep in that shed over yonder."

"I'll take it," replied Rex. "How many days a week do we work?"

"As many as you want. There's enough work to do around here that we never catch up."

"Then I'll work ever'day 'til you run me off. I need to git back on my feet after them ol' boys robbed me."

"Well, we can use you 'til Labor Day, at least, and maybe a week or two past that, too."

Rex worked the rest of the summer for the farmer and sometime after Labor Day returned, by a different route, far from Wichita, to Claremore. It should be noted that if a bulletin had been released regarding his escape from the road gang, he had given his name, when arrested with no identification documents, as Hiram Slade from Muskogee, Oklahoma.

Wanted In Wichita

Sit down here boy and I'll tell you a tale
How I escaped from the Wichita jail
Me 'n' my partner like a couple of fools
Got ourselves busted by the Wichita bulls
We rode the railroad and we didn't pay
The judge and the sheriff said "boys 30 days"
The men on the road gang they eat pretty well
Or take bread and water alone in your cell

I took the road gang my friend took the cell
I've got to admit he was lazy as hell
Me I'm a worker a gambler by trade
The slickest damned Okie that God ever made
I said to my buddy the food ain't that bad
Hell this ain't the worst job that I ever had
He said I ain't workin' on nobody's crew
I'll take bread and water...let's see how you do

The second day out we were clearin' thick brush
The sun it was hot the work it was tough
I said to the Cap'n I need some relief
He set down his shotgun and tossed me the keys
He said there's a thicket just over that hill
You've got five minutes and five more to kill
If you ain't back here to help roll out these logs
I'll figure you're runnin' and turn loose the dogs

I walked to the top of the hill like a man
As soon as I got out of vision I ran
I'd seen the highway when they brought us in
I measured the distance and ran like the wind
I threw out my thumb to a truck load of hay

The driver pulled over and wished me good day
We rode it as hard as that old truck would go
'til we reached Lyons Kansas and left 'em our load

I bid my old hay haulin' buddy adieu
I worked in the wheat 'til the harvest was through
By then I had money enough to compete
I went back to Claremore to the dust and the heat
Now I've often thought of my freight-hoppin' friend
I never heard from him or saw him again
I left for Modesto with the first winter's freeze
In the year of our Lord...Nineteen Thirty-Three

Words & Music by Gary Rex Tanner

Songs from this book can be heard at
www.oklahomagamblinman.com

To hear songs written & performed by Gary Rex Tanner
Please visit www.garyrextanner.com

15

Elmer Gantry Eat Your Heart Out

Back in Claremore Rex sought out his two brothers. Morris, he learned from Frank, had joined a Citizen's Conservation Corp camp in Arizona. Miller and the gamblers had not returned and Frank immediately informed Rex of another development.

"They got Kilmer over at the jail in Tulsa," he said.

"No shit, Frank," Rex exclaimed. "What'd they git 'im for?...Shit, I thought he got religion."

"Well, if he did," answered Frank, "he's preachin' it to them cons over in Tulsa. They got 'im for counterfeiting."

"Counterfeiting? You mean he was printing money?"

"Naw, he showed up back in Claremore after he left and was gone for a while with that tent revival preacher fella. He was drunk over at Mac's place one night and paid for whatever he bought with four or five fifty-cent pieces. Ol' Mac had one of his stooges runnin' the place and he didn't notice, or was afraid to say anything, that the coins were phonies." Frank went on, "When Mac was fixin' to take the night's take over to the bank the next day, he noticed the bad coins and asked his man who used them? Well, the guy told 'im it was Kilmer and Mac went over to Kilmer's hotel room and asked 'im to replace them with 'real' money. Kilmer got nasty with Mac and told 'im to pass them along to some of his backwoods customers and when Mac bucked up, Kilmer threatened to cut 'im. That really pissed Mac off and he went straight to Elmer with the coins and demanded Elmer arrest 'im."

"What'd Elmer do?" asked Rex.

"Elmer told 'im that he didn't have any jurisdiction over counterfeiting; that's a Federal offense. He told Mac that if he really wanted to press charges he'd have to go to Tulsa and see the Feds."

"Shit, Frank, he went to Tulsa over a couple of bucks?"

"Reckon he did. A day or two later the FBI come to town, arrested Kilmer and took 'im back to Tulsa."

"Well, shit, why'n't Elmer just give 'im the two bucks? Shit, man, Kilmer shouldn't be in jail over two bucks."

"Elmer don't give a shit about Kilmer…or you and me, neither," said Frank. "He thinks we're an embarrassment to the family…where you been, anyway?"

"Aw I uz over in Lyons, Kansas, workin' on a farm."

"You back now? There ain't much to do around here anymore, what with this Depression and all."

"I reckon I'm back…for now. Why'd Morris join the CCC boys?"

"He got tired of not eatin', I'd say," replied Frank.

"He's over in Arizona. Effie gits a letter from 'im

once in a while."

"Morris can write a letter? I'd like to see that."

"Well, shit, Rex, just 'cause we never went to school much don't mean Effie didn't teach us how to write. You read the newspaper ever'day…or at least you used to…don't you?"

"Yeah, I still do sometimes. I learned myself how to read better after the neighbors quit takin' me 'n' Morris to school. I reckon Effie did try to help us read and write better. I can read most anything but I cain't spell nothin' and no one can read what I do write."

"Well, you didn't need anyone to teach you how to cipher; you're like me and the old man. I reckon that's what makes you a good domino player."

"All right then," said Rex, "I need to go see Kilmer. Do you reckon they'll let anyone go visit 'im?"

"I think Fayette's been over to see 'im; why'n't y'all go over and see 'im and see how it works."

"I reckon I will dreckly. I ain't seen Fayette for a year or two, anyway. I bet he feels bad thinkin' Kilmer took up with that preacher and got religion."

"Well, tell Fayette I'll be out to see 'im 'fore long and if they let you visit Kilmer, tell 'im I hope they let 'im out soon."

Rex paid his uncle Fayette a visit and got the information on how to visit Kilmer at the Federal facility in Tulsa. Rex jumped the freight train, as he usually did, noticing that the numbers of free-riders had multiplied considerably since he'd last rode the train. When he was at the facility he was allowed to visit Kilmer in a small private room.

"Hey cousin," said Kilmer, entering the room.

"Kilmer," said Rex, somewhat uncomfortable with the surroundings.

"How'd workin' in the wheat turn out for you?" asked Kilmer.

"Better'n religion did for you, judgin' from what I been hearin'."

"Well, you cain't believe ever' thang you hear."

"Now that's a damn fact. What the hell happened, anyway?"

"Well, I tell you what, Rex, I ain't told nobody exactly what happened but you went to the trouble of comin' over here to see me, so I'm gonna give it to ya straight from the horse's mouth. Now what I tell ya is between you and me. You ain't to tell nobody else none of it…and I ain't gonna tell you all of it, but here she goes. I told you me 'n' that preacher hit it off right off the bat. 'Bout the second revival meetin' I went to, they was people screamin' and runnin' up and down the aisles, confessin' their sins and beggin' God to forgive 'em. The preacher picked out two pretty good lookin' young gals and told them their sins was forgiven and to come out to his trailer after the service. He had me bring 'im the money that had been collected and the four of us sat for a while and talked about the Lord. After about half an hour, the preacher got out a bottle of Scotch whiskey and poured us all a drink and offered a toast to Jesus. The young girls didn't mind drinkin' the whiskey with the preacher and 'fore it was over me 'n' the preacher each had our way with 'em. We repeated that a few times with different young gals and then me 'n' the preacher rolled it up and went to California. Now I always owned a .38 revolver and the preacher told me to bring it. When we got to California me 'n' him, after the revival services, took the collection money and spent it on whiskey, dope and whores. Man, Rex, some of them whores in California look like movie stars. Anyway, the money from the collections wasn't enough to cover everything we was doin' so me 'n' the preacher went out ever' night after the services and robbed gas stations and grocery stores. Hell, we must've robbed places from Los Angeles all the way up to Sacramento, mostly up the coast."

"Jesus, Kilmer, did anyone git hurt?"

"Shit, I don't really remember. I might of pistol whipped a couple of people and one time the clerk shot at us as we went out the door and the preacher emptied his gun shootin' back at 'im."

"Lucky you didn't git kilt."

"Well, here it is," Kilmer continued, "we uz at these cabins in a town called Stockton. Me 'n' the preacher each had two whores apiece. Now I think the preacher's whores was a mother, looked to be about thirty years old, and her young daughter, maybe fourteen or so. We checked in separately so nobody knowed we was together. I took my two whores and went into my cabin and the preacher did likewise. Now the preacher liked to rough the women up a bit and most of 'em didn't seem to mind too much, as long as they got the money. After I'd been doin' business with my whores for about an hour, I heard some screamin' comin' from the cabin next door where the preacher was. I didn't think much of it at the time; hell, he was always makin' whores cry and yellin' and carryin' on, but I heard a car start up and drive off and I went to see what was goin' on. When I looked outside, the preacher's car was gone and the door to his cabin was open. I walked over and looked in and it didn't look like no one was there. I thought, *Shit, that son of a bitch drove off with them two whores and left me here afoot.* I walked through the door and then I seen 'im on the other side of the bed, on the floor. I went over to where he was layin' and saw his throat was cut and he was dead as a doornail. There was blood ever'where and all his money and jewelry was gone. I thought, *Shit, I better git the hell out of here 'fore someone thinks I done it.* I went back where I'd left my two whores and they was gone and so was all my money, my gun and my jewelry. The only thing I found was a small bank bag with thirty or forty counterfeit fifty-cent pieces. I thought, *Who in the hell would be dumb enough to spend the time makin' counterfeit fifty-cent pieces*?"

"Jesus Christ, Kilmer," Rex interjected, "how'd they git there?"

"I reckon them whores must've had 'em and after stealing my money and my gun, figgered they didn't need 'em anymore. Anyway, I was afoot, the preacher was dead in the other cabin and when I went back over there I saw his gun was gone, too. I had no car, no gun, no money, no whores…no shit! I hot-wahred a car in the parkin' lot and drove to a town called Modesto, about thirty miles away. I parked that car and stole some ol' boy's Cadillac and switched it with a new Chevrolet in Bakersfield. From there I made it to Lordsburg, New Mexico, where I got some Mexican, who said he wasn't a Mexican, to give me fifty dollars for it, and I stole another car and drove it from there to Tulsa, where I finally knowed someone. I sold that car for enough to eat and git back to Claremore and by the time I got back and found a whore and got drunk, all I had left was them God damn fifty cent pieces."

"Shit, Kilmer," reasoned Rex, "maybe you'd a been better off really gittin' religion."

"That ain't funny, Rex, but I reckon that's prob'ly a true statement, cousin. If I'd a knowed all that was gonna happen, I prob'ly would've. So when I didn't give ol' Mac back his two dollars, he went to Elmer, who sent 'im here to Tulsa, and here we are."

"What's gonna happen now?" asked Rex.

"Well, they're a tellin' me the judge can give me twenty-five years over in Leavenworth if I'm found guilty. They got the evidence and I cain't really tell 'em about how I got them coins, so I'm thinkin' about takin' what they're callin' a plea deal."

"What's that?"

"Well, they say if I plead guilty, they'll give me ten to fifteen years and iffen I don't cause any trouble while I'm in the pen, it'll be closer to ten."

"Jesus Christ Kilmer, fifteen years for TWO DOLLARS?"

"Naw, it ain't two dollars, cousin," said Kilmer quietly, "it's ever' thang evil I ever done. I'm sure I got the time comin'…I been dodgin' this bullet most of my life."

Rex didn't bother telling Kilmer about Wichita; it hardly compared with anything Kilmer had just told him. After more conversation the time was up and the two cousins shook hands and the jailer led Kilmer back to his cell. A few weeks later Kilmer made the plea bargain and spent his next ten years in Leavenworth Federal Penitentiary.

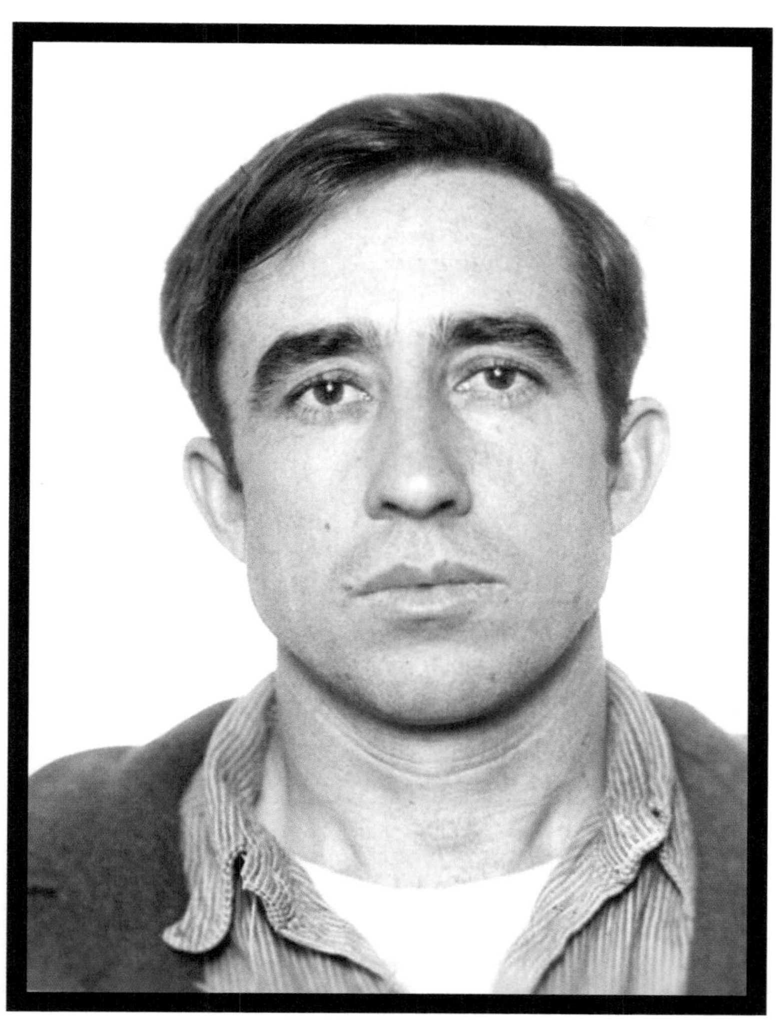

Kilmer Tanner 1933

Fayette's Boys

When Buster and Elwood and Kilmer were boys
They raised holy hell and they made lots of noise
Their pa was a preacher who tended his flock
But his three sons were never chips off the old block

Roe dee oh doe dee oh doe roe dee oh doe dee oh

They say that old Buster would fight a buzz saw
That he never once swung that a man didn't fall
He'd fight you for money he'd fight you for fun
Then he'd buy you a drink when the fightin' was done

Roe dee oh doe dee oh doe roe dee oh doe dee oh

Now some say that Elwood was a brick or two shy
Of a load 'cause he had a strange look in his eye
He was just a mere boy when he wandered from home
And everyone said he was best left alone

Roe dee oh doe dee oh doe roe dee oh doe dee oh

Now Kilmer was mean from the time of his birth
Spent ten years breakin' rocks in Leavenworth
He fought with a knife and he robbed with a gun
But they got him for somethin' that he never done

Roe dee oh doe dee oh doe roe dee oh doe dee oh

Well I know Fayette's boys are all doin' just fine
Though they've been gone from this world for a time
I know when I hear thunder crack in the air
They're raisin' hell up there in heaven somewhere

Roe dee oh doe dee oh doe roe dee oh doe dee oh

Words by Gary Rex Tanner
Music: Sweet Betsy From Pike Traditional

Songs from this book can be heard at
www.oklahomagamblinman.com

To hear songs written & performed by Gary Rex Tanner
Please visit www.garyrextanner.com

16

California Here I Come

Rex returned to Claremore and scuffled around the domino parlor, made a few deliveries for Frank and generally laid low. This was the longest Miller and the gamblers had been away since he'd begun working for them three years earlier. Times had changed; the Depression was taking a toll on everything. Prohibition had been repealed earlier that year, but not in Oklahoma. Oklahoma had a unique position regarding prohibition. It was the only state that had written prohibition laws into its state constitution when it entered the union in 1907. The rest of the country didn't enforce prohibition until 1920. When prohibition was repealed in 1933, Oklahoma kept it in force until 1953. The original idea for enacting prohibition in Oklahoma was to keep liquor out of the hands of the disproportionately large Indian population. After it was in force for a time, illegal liquor became such a lucrative industry in Oklahoma for those who participated in it that they were able to lobby local politicians to keep it going. Will Rogers once wryly remarked, "Oklahoma will remain a dry state for as long as its citizens can stagger to the polls."

A few days after his return from Tulsa, Rex was sitting at the counter of the small café where he usually ate breakfast. While he was waiting for his order to come, a middle-aged man in a wrinkled suit took the seat next to him. It was obvious to Rex that the man wasn't from the area and when the man caught Rex glancing at him, he asked, "Are you Rex Tanner?"

"Reckon I am," replied Rex.

The man reached for his jacket pocket, pulled out an identification card and said, "I'm Agent Phillips of the FBI."

Rex stiffened and tried to remain calm. His mind immediately thought of Wichita and the thought of having to go back there, or worse, sickened his stomach and killed his appetite.

"Well, it's a pleasure to know you, Agent Phillips," Rex replied, with his best poker face. "What are you havin' for breakfast this mornin'?"

"How about we slide into that booth over there?" Phillips motioned. "I've got something I'd like to ask you."

"All right," said Rex, moving toward the booth.

Once they were seated, the G-man looked Rex over thoroughly and asked, "How old are you?"

"Twenty years old."

"Jesus, I thought you'd be older."

"Well, lots of people take me for bein' older."

"OK, let me begin. Do you know a man by the name of Vernon Miller?"

"Naw, I never heard of nobody like that."

"Well, how about Bernard Phillips?" the G-man went on.

"Naw, him neither."

The agent went through a list of names; Rex denied ever having heard of any of them. Rex had regained his appetite by now, learning that none of this had anything to do with Wichita. Now it was like he was playing dominos: he measured each move and calculated the moves his opponent might bring to the table.

His breakfast came and he began to eat.

"All right, tell me what you know about a gambling operation operating out of the Claremore Hotel?"

"I wouldn't know nothin' about anything like that. Hell, I don't even gamble."

The agent looked long and hard at Rex, deliberately pausing to allow his facial expression and what he was about to say to make an impact in its most profound way on this cool young hustler.

"OK, son," the agent continued, "I want you to listen carefully. I'm going to give you some really good advice. If you're smart, you'll follow it. I've spoken with your Uncle Elmer; he's cooperating with our investigation. The FBI was created to put an end to these vicious gangsters that have been terrorizing the Midwest the past few years. J. Edgar Hoover has pledged to rid the country of these outlaws, and in the next couple of years they're all going to be dead or in jail. I understand your cousin Kilmer's on his way to Leavenworth."

"That's a bum rap," replied Rex, "fifteen years for two dollars."

"We're gonna nail 'em any way we can. Capone's going down for tax evasion."

"I don't know what that means. I ain't never made enough money to pay any taxes."

"Well, what it means is, if I was you, I'd be lookin' for someplace to light, where nobody knows you. There's folks leavin' out of here every day for California and Florida and other parts unknown. Elmer says you're a good kid; I'll take him at his word. The people you've been associating with are in a lot of trouble…you may be, too. Now as far as I'm concerned, if I never see you again, I'll probably forget we ever had this talk…You might want to think about what I'm saying."

With that, the FBI agent rose from his seat and walked out the door.

Rex calmly finished his breakfast, ordered another cup of coffee, smoked a cigarette and tried to absorb what this man had just told him. Leaving the café, he found Jack Burns, on whom he knew he could always count. He told Jack of his conversation with the FBI agent and about Wichita. Jack had a good car and suggested they make a trip out to California and test the waters. That night, after telling Effie, Frank and his sisters goodbye, they headed for the CCC camp to pick up Morris, who Rex knew would be game for anything he wanted to try. When they got to the camp Jack waited outside the campgrounds with the motor running while Rex went in to find Morris. Within fifteen minutes Rex and Morris returned, carrying a duffle bag full of Morris' belongings, and the trip to California began.

Morris Tanner (circa 1933)

The Oklahoma Gamblin' Man

He grew up in the shadows of Bonnie & Clyde
Bootleggin' whiskey...shootin' pool on the side
Hustlin' suckers with his bank robber friends
Dealin' in card games where nobody wins

Who's the man behind the mask
What's that up his sleeve you ask
Keep your eyes on the hands
Of the Oklahoma gamblin' man

Pretty Boy Floyd came through one night
Lookin' for cover...travelin' light
The FBI wanted him dead
But the local police just went to bed

He passed through clean the story goes
Next day who shows up in his clothes
I'll be damned...
The Oklahoma gamblin' man

Miller's workin' on a plan
We need another steady hand
We could use a man like you
Who drives a car the way you do

They robbed 'em a bank across the Kansas state line
But he wouldn't go...he said "Maybe next time"
But them ol' boys had gone one bank too far
Now the cops was right on 'em shootin' holes in their car

A G-man shows up back in town
Askin' questions all around
He's got a plan
For the Oklahoma gamblin' man

They tell me you're a gambler son
But you're just a kid not even twenty-one
If you just kind of disappear
I'll probably forget that you were ever here

Out in California you can cut a fat pig
Okies out there are makin' it big
Do you understand
Mr Oklahoma gamblin' man...
I said do you understand...
Mr Oklahoma gamblin' man

Words & Music by Gary Rex Tanner

Songs from this book can be heard at
www.oklahomagamblinman.com

To hear songs written & performed by Gary Rex Tanner
Please visit www.garyrextanner.com

California
Chico
Lake Tahoe
Placerville
Sacramento
Berkeley
Stockton
San Francisco
Tracy
Modesto
Turlock
San Jose
Merced
Fresno
Monterey
Salinas
Hanford
Visalia
San Luis Obispo
Bakersfield
Los Angeles
San Bernardino
Riverside

17

California Pie

The drive to California took about two days and nights. It was a chilly mid-autumn and Jack's car, while dependable, didn't have a heater. Although many Midwesterners were migrating to California, leaving farms and ranches that had been devastated by the "dust-bowl" conditions, the heaviest numbers would not depart for a couple of more years. When the men crossed the state line from Arizona, they saw a large billboard that read: "Keep California Green!"

"Keep California Green?" said Jack. "What does that mean?"

"Don't tell 'em nothin'," joked Morris, "don't tell 'em nothin'."

The three men didn't have a clear destination and followed the highway, stopping along the way, sizing up the terrain and asking questions about work, lodging, etc.

MODESTO
WATER WEALTH CONTENTMENT HEALTH

"Most Okies are going up to the San Joaquin Valley," said one old timer in San Bernardino. "There's lots of agriculture work up there."

"I worked on a farm in Kansas," said Rex. "Reckon I could do whatever agriculture work they got. What kind of work is that, anyway?"

"You know, son," said the man, "pickin' fruit and vegetables and the like."

The men were given a road map at a filling station and decided to travel up Highway 99 through Bakersfield, Fresno and north to Sacramento. When they got to a town called Modesto, they were just about out of money and decided to try to find work and at least temporarily establish themselves. By now they'd heard the epithet "Okies" several times and realized that they weren't exactly welcomed, or respected, by the natives. Jack was a little insulted by the term, but Rex and Morris thought it was quite humorous and began to refer to themselves and each other as such.

"What did one Okie say to the other Okie as they was comin' across the state line from Arizona?" joked Morris.

"Hell, I don't know," said Jack.

"Keep California green, boy...keep California green!" laughed Morris, repeatedly. "Don't tell 'em nothin'."

The second day in Modesto, Rex got lucky and found employment at an ice plant. The boys had rented a room downtown, and the next day he was able to get Jack a job there, too. Morris familiarized himself with the town, asked about employment and learned about the times of year laborers were hired to work the crops. Rex and Jack learned to drag huge blocks of ice around the plant, cut them into smaller blocks and load them on trucks to be delivered to homes that needed ice for their ice boxes.

"That's some backbreakin' work for two dollars a day," said Jack after the first day.

"Beats not eatin'," said Rex. "We'll find somethin'

better dreckly."

A few days passed and Morris had learned that not much happened as far as hiring "Okies" to work the crops until spring.

Jack became discouraged and after a couple of weeks decided to return to Claremore. Morris had been receiving letters from a girlfriend he had left behind when he joined the CCC camp and decided for now, since there was little work to be found, he would accompany Jack back to Claremore and perhaps return at a later date. Rex didn't really have the option of returning to Claremore and since he had a job where his employers seemed to like him and treated him with respect, he decided to go it alone. It would prove to be a difficult winter for Rex. The weather was cold and foggy and the ten or so hours a day in the bitter cold of the ice plant was depressing. Years later he would remark that if it had been heat, rather than the cold from the weather and the ice, he'd have believed he'd gone to hell.

Having not heard from Morris or Jack, Rex called Claremore and was able to reach Frank by phone at the taxi stand. Frank told him that Miller's body had been found strangled by the side of a road in Michigan, near Detroit. Frank didn't know anything else about it, just what he had heard through the bootleggers' grapevine. He also told Rex that Pretty Boy Floyd had been killed and that he had attended his funeral.

"He wasn't wearin' my cashmere sweater, was he?" asked Rex.

Frank laughed, "Naw, he was wearin' a suit like the one he gave you."

"Well, I don't reckon he's got much use for a sweater now anyway," Rex laughed. "Prob'ly ain't gonna be too cold where he's goin'"

"They got Dillinger, too," Frank continued. "Them FBI boys are all over eastern Oklahoma these days. Things have really slowed down around here. It's a good thing Oklahoma didn't decide to overturn Prohibition like the rest of the country. Otherwise I wouldn't have nothin' to do."

"So did Morris and Jack make it back ok? I ain't heard nothin' from 'em since they left here."

"Yeah, I seen 'em both a couple of days ago."

"Is Morris goin' back to the CCC camp?"

"I don't think so. He's been scuffling around Claremore looking for work with the old man and I don't think he's gonna leave his girlfriend ag'in."

"How 'bout Jack? What's he doin'?"

"I hardly ever run into 'im but he always seems to manage to stay busy with somethin'."

"How are Effie and the girls?"

"They're fine. I been keepin' an eye on 'em."

"Well, if you ever git tard of sellin' whiskey to Indians, come on out here to California and we'll pick some prunes."

"Well, you never know, maybe I will someday."

"All right then, you take care and give Effie my best."

"Ok, you too, bye."

Rex realized that he didn't know much about what was going on in the country. In Oklahoma he more or less absorbed the news by word of mouth and what he heard on the radio. He began to read the newspaper every day, as he had in earlier years. One Saturday afternoon, having been given the rest of the day off at the ice plant, he wandered downtown a few blocks from the boarding house on Eleventh Street, where he had rented the room with Jack and Morris, who by now had been gone a few months. He paid a quarter for a ticket to a movie at the Strand Theater on Tenth Street. In those days, before the main film began, or between features, if there was a double feature, the theater showed a newsreel, usually with news that was a couple of weeks old. Suddenly upon the screen came a lineup of men whom the narrator's voice from the newsreel announced had been apprehended for robbing banks in Kansas and Oklahoma. There was Bernie and three or four of the other men that Rex had worked with at various times at the "casino." Now it became crystal clear what Bernie had meant about a "little trip," and why Kilmer had advised him to refrain from joining them. Miller was dead; Bernie and the other men were in jail, as was Kilmer. He wondered if Quick Johnny was still in the Wichita jail. In the spring he left the ice plant and tried his hand at picking fruit. He wasn't too bad at picking peaches, and he could make five dollars a day if the trees were well laden. People were saying that with the bad economy and all the Okies coming in, things were going to get tighter and tighter. Rex missed Claremore, but he knew he wasn't ever going to live there again.

STRAND
THEATRE
STRAND

Oklahoma On My Mind

Got no time and I got no money
Guess I'll see you later honey
I've got Oklahoma on my mind
California's got a nice coast line
The sun keeps shinin' and the weather's fine
But I've got Oklahoma on my mind
I went busted and learned my lesson
It may not show but I'm confessin'
I've got Oklahoma on my mind
My cousin Kilmer's lookin' through steel bars
I'm out here with the movie stars
And I've got Oklahoma on my mind

Two thousand miles from home
Lost and broke and all alone
I may be down but I swear by God
I'm gonna get up on my own

Met a fella just the other day
Plays country music in a different way
He's got Oklahoma on his mind
Me 'n' him we don't think the same
He wants to change the rules I'm tryin' to win the game
But we've got Oklahoma on our minds

Took a trip down to Mexico
Tried to find some Spanish gold
I had Oklahoma on my mind
They took my money and they took my shoes
I walked home whistlin' the Bad Luck Blues
Still had Oklahoma on my mind

Turned my back on a life of crime
Left my gamblin' ways behind
All that's left is to figure out
What California's all about

Kissed my mama and I hugged the rest
Picked up Morris and I headed west
We had California on our minds
If you ever see me comin' back
I'll be drivin' a Cadillac
And I'll have Oklahoma off my mind

All these good ol' boys I meet
In the bars and on the street
They've got Oklahoma on their minds
For me the past has turned to dust
The life I had has gone to rust
And I've got Oklahoma on my mind

Got no time and I've got no money
Guess I'll see you later honey
I've got Oklahoma on my mind
California's got a nice coastline
The sun keeps shinin' and the weather's fine
But I've got Oklahoma on my mind

Words & Music by Gary Rex Tanner

Elmer Tanner 1912

18

Attacked By Indians

Back in Claremore things had slowed down noticeably for Frank. The repeal of Prohibition had made it easy to bring in liquor from newly established "wet" states. Still, running the taxi stand and selling bootleg whiskey enabled Frank to own his own car and live relatively well. Frank always saved most of his money, so he wasn't too worried about the future. Morris had returned to Claremore, but Frank missed Kilmer and his younger brother Rex. One night, in the middle of the week, Frank was preparing to close up the stand, which stood outside the storefront where the cab company's office was located, when a dark, threatening figure came out of the shadows and addressed him.

"Frank Tannuh…I needs a pint o' that rotgut whiskey you's a sellin'." It was Harm Slade, and he was in a contentious mood.

"I sold my last pint a couple of hours ago, Harm,"

Frank replied. "I won't have nothin' 'til tomorra afternoon."

"Don't give me that shit," growled Harm. "You always got somethin' laid back for dem crackuh frens o' yourn…Bring out a pint or me 'n' you's fixin' to git real personal heah, boy."

Frank stiffened and then relaxed. He knew Harm and his reputation. He'd sold whiskey to him before and had never had any trouble with him. But this wasn't the Harm he'd done business with previously, and he leveled a cold hard eye at the menacing figure before him as he stepped from behind the taxi stand with his Barlow hidden behind his right leg, clutched like an ice pick with the blade facing down from his fist and toward its potential target. Kilmer had taught Frank that if ever you had to fight for your life with a knife, never to "stab" your adversary. "It's better to slash and try to cut a leader," Kilmer had said. "A man cut bad gets weaker as he loses blood, and the sight of his own blood usually causes 'im to lose heart." Additionally, Kilmer had said, "You might stick somebody in the gut or chest and he'll die an hour later; in the meantime, he's still got strength enough to kill you."

Frank knew Harm was left-handed, and standing about five feet away, he remained focused on Harm's left shoulder. Sure enough, Harm brought his left hand behind him to remove the razor from its home in his back pocket. But before he could bring it to daylight, the Barlow had struck, cutting Harm's left arm to the bone from the middle of his left tricep to the middle of his left bicep.

"Why you son of a bitch," Harm hollered, "I'm gonna cut your heart out."

Frank wasted no breath with a retort and as Harm discovered he'd lost motion of his left arm, he reached across his body to take up the razor with his right hand. As he did so, the Barlow found the bottom of his right cheekbone and cut its way up to his eyebrow, which almost immediately rendered Harm half-blind. Still, Harm was a powerful man and enraged to a point where he was able to bring forth strength uncommon in an ordinary man. Harm began to slash at Frank right-handed, nicking him a couple of times on the left side. Then Frank did the unexpected: instead of continuing to circle right to Harm's blind side, he quickly stepped forward, chest to chest, taking away Harm's ability to slash at his exposed body and allowing him to bring the Barlow up from Harm's groin to his left nipple. Now Frank was in position to easily cut Harm's throat. He'd finished off a hundred hogs in that manner, but something deep inside told him that if he did, he might suffer for it at a later date. Instead, he took two or three of Harm's razor slashes to his left buttocks and lower back and punched Harm in the Adam's apple, which caused the Barlow to cut Harm again at the sternum. Harm was weak by now and Frank pushed him backward. Harm was two-hundred-twenty pounds and Frank weighed one-hundred-sixty, fully clothed, but Frank's forward momentum and Harm's weakened condition caused him to stagger backward and slowly sink, sitting down, against the outer wall of the taxi company office. Frank was bleeding badly, too, but remained standing, not trusting Harm not to suddenly jump up and rush him. Harm's eyes were becoming glassy as he lost more blood. Frank's right buttock, uncut, found the stool that he sometimes sat on as he dispatched cabs. He leaned heavily on the counter of the taxi stand, with the Barlow still firmly clutched in his hand, keeping a watchful eye on Harm. Several minutes passed, and the cab that Frank had been waiting for arrived. The driver, seeing the bleeding, helpless men, jumped out of his cab and ran to the phone and called an ambulance and the police. Frank and Harm were taken together to the hospital, where Harm was given a transfusion and a morphine drip. Frank allowed his wounds to be stitched, but refused blood and declined painkillers. The two men were placed in a room together, with their beds side by side, lying quietly, Harm unconscious and Frank staring at the ceiling, until Elmer arrived.

"God damn Frank," Elmer bellowed, upon arriving. "Are you crazy? Cuttin' up a nigger right on the street after we all just got over them race riots over in Tulsa fifteen years ago?"

"Don't call 'im no nigger, and I didn't cut 'im," Frank replied calmly.

"You didn't cut 'im?" Elmer screamed. "Shit-fahr, boy, look at 'im; he's cut six ways from Sunday!"

"Well, he may be," Frank answered, "and so am I. But I never had nothin' to do with it."

"Well, then you tell me," Elmer demanded, "what do you say happened?"

"Well," Frank began, "I was gittin' ready to close up and Harm there come up and asked me if I could git 'im a taxi to take 'im over to Muskogee, which I'd done many times before. I said I'd try to and as I was fixin' to contact my last driver that was out, a couple of Indians walked up and tried to rob us."

"Are you shittin' me?" yelled Elmer, turning around to try to make eye contact with whoever might be listening nearby.

As Elmer turned, Frank caught Harm's right eye staring at him as though he had heard the conversation that was taking place.

"'Attacked by Indians!?' For Christ's sake, that takes the God damn cake. I'm tellin' you, Frank," continued Elmer, "it ain't bad enough your daddy's the God damn town drunk and Kilmer's gone to Leavenworth and Rex had to leave town in the middle of the night. You people are a God damn embarrassment and a disgrace to the Tanner family. Attacked by Indians!? That's about the stupidest God damn thing I ever heard. You're plumb crazy if you think I'm buyin' that story. So tell me, Frank, Harm's holdin' a straight razor when we get to the taxi stand and the doctor here says you been cut with a straight razor. How do you explain that?"

"The Indians had straight razors," explained Frank.

"Indians with straight razors?" Elmer yelled with disbelief. "Indians don't carry straight razors, you dumb son of a bitch, they carry tomahawks!"

Hurt as he was, Frank could barely keep from laughing.

"What was Harm cut with?" asked Frank.

"We don't know yet. We're figurin' it's that Barlow you carry."

"Naw, I don't carry no knife. Did you find a knife at the taxi stand?"

"You know God damn well we didn't find no knife there," a frustrated Elmer replied, "'cause you know what you did with it."

"Shit, Elmer, cut as I am, how could I git rid of somethin' as big as a knife that you think I have?"

"Well, that's a mystery I intend to solve," promised Elmer, "and when I do, you ain't gonna like it much."

"You ain't gonna find nothin'...unless you find them two Indians that attacked us," said Frank.

Elmer turned to the doctor that had just walked into the room. "I want you to turn these two beds around facin' each other, so's these two 'Indian Fighters' can be reminded of what happens when you go against the law."

With that, Elmer turned and swiftly walked out of the room and out into the cold spring Oklahoma night.

Frank spent the next three days lying in his hospital bed facing Harm, always keeping a watchful eye open for a sudden movement or an unexpected visitor. Effie and Frank's younger sisters came by to visit him; his oldest sister Iva had moved to Michigan and their sister Ruth had died giving birth to her first child a few years earlier. Frank advised them to tell Leonard not to come to the hospital, fearing some kind of altercation if or when he encountered Harm. Harm was still on the morphine and spent most of the time asleep or being taken to the toilet by the male nurse's aides.

After three days, Frank got up, put on his clothes and walked out of the hospital. No one tried to stop him as he limped out the hospital's front entrance and into the cab that was waiting for him. Frank didn't trust Elmer. There was bad blood between them, especially now, after the things Elmer had said to him. Frank felt Elmer could have saved Kilmer from going to Leavenworth by giving the Scotsman two dollars. To Frank that meant none of Leonard's or Fayette's family were worth two dollars to Elmer. Additionally, Frank knew that there was potential for an attempt at retribution, should Harm choose to continue the dispute. Frank was easy to find in Claremore and his main ally, Kilmer, was long gone. So was Rex.

Frank pondered his next move for a couple of days, then went to see Effie, Leonard and his sisters and announced he was leaving to go stay with sister Iva in Michigan for a while. Frank always had money and his car, while not a showpiece like Miller and the gamblers drove, was sturdy and dependable. He loaded up what belongings he thought would be needed; gave the rest to Morris and Leonard and then drove straight to California. When he got to Modesto, Rex was waiting for him. Rex advised him of the local scene and conditions and Frank related to Rex what had happened in Claremore. Frank didn't stay in Modesto long, choosing to move farther west to the San Francisco Bay area, where he found employment as a stevedore down at the waterfront docks. No one but Rex knew where to find Frank and after a couple of weeks, Rex advised the kinfolk back in Claremore that Frank wouldn't be going to Michigan after all. Morris called Rex in Modesto to tell him to tell Frank that Harm had been released from the hospital. A few months later word was sent that Harm had died.

Leonard Franklin Tanner (Frank-circa 1935)

19

Jackpot!

One Saturday afternoon in Modesto, in the spring of 1935, Rex ducked in out of the rain at the Strand Theater, where he had viewed his former colleagues the year before. Buying a ticket, he absentmindedly took the quarter change from the half-dollar with which he'd paid for his ticket and bought a "raffle" ticket from an usher standing near the entrance of the theater. The theater regularly had promotions where they held a drawing during intermissions and drew one ticket from a large glass container filled with the money that had been paid for the raffle tickets. The theater took 10% and gave the winner the remainder of the money. There had been no winners for several days and the "pot" loomed impressively large, looking from the outside into the glass bowl. After the first feature the lights went on for intermission and a gentleman came on stage and began the drawing. Rex was sitting up in the balcony, where smoking was allowed, and wasn't paying much attention to the proceedings, impatient for the second feature to begin. The man announced the numbers of the ticket he had drawn. No one responded. He called the number out again and still no one responded. He announced that if no one answered the third call, the money would be added to the next day's pot, as it had been for several days. Rex yawned and glanced at his raffle ticket stub, which he had inadvertently pulled from his shirt pocket along with the package of Camels for his next smoke.

"Jesus Christ," Rex yelled from deep in the balcony seats, "I've got it! I've got the winning number!"

"Well, come on down, son," the announcer invited. "If you have the winning ticket, you've just won a nice jackpot."

Rex did indeed have the winning number and was given the money, less the 10%, which he loaded into every pocket in every piece of clothing he was wearing. Rex was heavy with the weight of quarters, half-dollars, dollars and a few two dollar bills as he walked the few blocks back to his boarding house room. When Rex got to his room he counted his swag and to his surprise and delight, he had more than eight hundred dollars. Rex didn't trust anyone where he lived and had no local friends. He locked himself in his room until the banks opened Monday morning, not even going out for meals. The next day Rex opened an account at a nearby bank and deposited the money. Up to this point Rex had not had many options in California, always being restricted by a lack of sufficient funds. His new-found fortune suddenly allowed his creative juices to flow and he quickly devised a plan that would begin to bring his family back together.

Later in the week, he made calls to Claremore, San Francisco and Michigan, setting up a family exodus from Oklahoma and a reunion in Modesto. He bought a 1928

Chevrolet sedan, which he drove to Claremore, loaded up Effie, three sisters and Ruby, Frank's fiancé, whom Frank had left behind when he fled to California. Leonard, his sister Effie Mae and the two little brothers went to Michigan to stay with Iva, who had opened and was operating a successful family restaurant in Standish, Michigan. Rex's sister Clarace had married and lived in Claremore with her husband and would join the family in Modesto at a later date.

Returning to California, the group now joined the heart of the Okie migration, an endless procession of beat-up, broken down vehicles overloaded with anything of value that could be transported. It was a much longer trip than when Rex, Jack and Morris had come two years earlier. Stopped at the Arizona state line, they were forced to pull over and wait with hundreds of other families while the state decided whether or not to allow them entrance, due to an alleged tuberculosis scare. Many vehicles, after waiting endless hours, simply turned around and returned to from whence they had come. It was the Depression all right… very depressing. When they were finally allowed to go on, they made it as far as Bakersfield, where they ran out of gas. Rex had spent every penny getting this far and none of the sisters, Effie, or Ruby had any money. Rex had pulled into a gas station and parked the car out of the traffic area. He rifled through the boxes crammed in the trunk of his car, trying to find something of value that might get him a tank of gas, which would almost certainly get them to Modesto. After going through a couple of boxes, he came upon the suit that Floyd had given him. Taking the suit up to the station attendant, he explained his predicament and offered to trade the obviously expensively tailored suit for a tank of gas, the cost of which was two or three dollars. The attendant hem-hawed around for a minute of two and then reluctantly agreed to make the transaction. Rex declined to advise the attendant on the origin of the suit.

When the group arrived in Modesto, late at night, the only place they had to stay was Rex's room at the boarding house. They all quietly spent the night there, and the next day Frank came over from San Francisco to pick up Ruby and paid the first month's rent on a modest house where Effie and the girls could stay. Rex took two sisters, and they found a job picking early peaches in a nearby town called Empire. Rex gave up his room at the boarding house and moved to the house that Frank had rented, with Effie and his sisters. Rex worked picking various fruit crops that summer, mainly peaches, plums and apricots. When winter began to set in, he returned to his job at the ice plant, which ironically was always slow in the winter months, but the owner sometimes had trouble finding workers who could tolerate the cold.

The winter of 1935 passed slowly, but now Rex had family nearby and felt a bit more connected. His employers at the ice plant understood when he chose not to work there when the weather warmed and he could make more money elsewhere. As summer rolled into fall and winter approached, Rex began to become restless for something more than being an agricultural worker and a mule at the ice plant.

Rex began to ask around about various employment opportunities.

"You might try catchin' on over at Gallo Wine," one acquaintance suggested.

"I reckon that might be a good idea now that there ain't no more prohibition," Rex replied.

Rex visited the winery to ask for work and was told to go over to the warehouse loading dock before 7am the next day and talk to the warehouse supervisor, who did most of the hiring and firing for the winery. Rex arrived a half-hour early and walked up the stairs to the loading dock and was greeted by an older gentleman with white hair and a ruddy complexion.

"You the driver I've been waiting for?" he said, before Rex could introduce himself.

"Reckon maybe I am," replied Rex, thinking there might be a job opening for someone to make deliveries.

"I've been waiting for your sorry ass for an hour and a half," the old man, who had obviously been "sampling" the load, said.

Suddenly, the conversation became a domino game to Rex and he carefully and quickly developed his strategy. "Sorry I'm late. I didn't know exactly what time to come in."

"That figures," said the dispatcher. "No one ever gets here on time these days."

"It won't happen ag'in," promised Rex. "I'm ready to work."

"All right then," said the dispatcher, "here's the manifest and a map to your destination in Los Angeles, and there's your truck. Take this load to the warehouse there on the paperwork, and they'll pay you and give you a bus ticket back to Modesto. There's a phone number there if you run into any trouble…maybe I'll see you when you get back."

Rex looked at the big semi-truck loaded with cases of wine and wondered if he might be biting off more than he could chew. It wasn't his nature to be intimidated by sudden challenges and so as the dispatcher turned and walked away; Rex walked to the truck, stepped up on the running board and opened the cab door. Rex wasn't sure exactly how the gear levers worked, but the truck was backed up to the loading dock and he figured he could move forward, which in a few minutes he did. Rex spent the next thirteen miles to Turlock figuring out the first gear box. When he got to Merced, thirty miles south of Modesto, he pulled into a truck stop and entered the coffee shop and took a seat at the counter. Two middle-aged gentlemen were having breakfast, and one of them looked over at Rex and said, "That your big rig out there?"

"Well, I'm drivin' it, if that's what you mean," said

GALLO
Daisy

Rex. "I'm takin' a load of Gallo wine up to Los Angeles."

"That's a long day," said the man. "We're goin' to Bakersfield with our load. I'm Phil and this is my brother Marvin."

"I'm proud to meet y'all. How long you boys been drivin' trucks?"

Phil looked at Marvin and said, "Ten years?"

"Yeah, probably," said Marvin, "maybe longer."

"Say," said Rex, "I wonder if you boys could show me how to git that truck out of that first low gear, gear box?"

"You're shittin' us, aren't you, Rex?" Phil replied with a grin.

"Naw…not really, it took me to Turlock to git out of low gear. Now that I figgered out how to git to the highest gear in the first box, I can only git up to about twenty miles an hour."

Marvin began to laugh heartily and Phil quickly joined him.

"No shit, Rex, you ain't never drove a semi truck before? Who hired you boy?" asked Phil. "You ever been up the grapevine?"

"Can't say I have. What's 'the grapevine'?"

"Jesus Christ," said Marvin, "we're gonna have to help this dumb bastard out, here…Rex, you gotta be crazy, but here's what we'll do. I'll drive your truck with you to Fresno and show you how to use the gear shifts and a bunch of other stuff you don't know. Then I'll ride with you while you drive to Bakersfield and we'll stop to eat at the truck stop. After we eat, you can go on up the grapevine to LA and me 'n' Phil will take our load to where we're goin'."

Rex was grateful for the help his two new friends were offering him. He began to think about how he might have fared if he had not by chance met them. This wasn't by far the tightest pinch Rex had been in during his twenty-three years. Still he recognized the value of the aid they were giving him.

"Hey fellas, that's mighty kind of you. I reckon I'll have a better chance of makin' that 'grapevine' than I would have if I hadn't run on to you boys. I shore wish there was some way I could make this up to y'all."

"Yeah, Rex," said Phil, "I don't know what you were thinking taking that load from Gallo without ever having drove a semi before."

"Yeah, I can see what you're a sayin'," said Rex, "but where I come from we look at things a little different than you boys do. Maybe after I git paid I'll look for a different kind of job."

Rex listened carefully to Marvin's instructions as he drove the truck to Fresno. They exchanged places and Rex drove the rig to Bakersfield, where Marvin and Phil bought his dinner and wished him well. Rex made it to the warehouse on the map after midnight and parked the rig in the big asphalt parking area in front of the locked gate and slept in the cab. At 6am he was awakened from his sleep by a gentleman who signed off on his load. Rex declined the offer of waiting for a load to take back to Modesto. He got his twenty dollars for the job, along with the Greyhound bus ticket back to Modesto, and never returned to Gallo Winery looking for work.

More than three decades later, while having lunch with Ernest Gallo and his brother Julio's son Bob, Rex would relate this story and share a long hearty laugh with them.

20

The Girl From Missouri

Rex walked into the café where he usually ate when he wasn't working. It was early spring of nineteen thirty-six. He immediately noticed the pretty young girl behind the counter, who had never before been there. Taking a seat at the counter, he picked up a menu and began to study the specials

"Hello," the pretty girl said cheerfully.

"Hi," said Rex, trying to think of something to extend the conversation.

"That hot roast beef sandwich is good today," she offered.

"That sounds good. I'll have that."

Although Rex had seven sisters and had worked with the whores in Claremore, he wasn't skilled or comfortable breaking the ice with pretty young women. He thought hard to come up with something to say that might interest this

DeLois Bowles Tanner

friendly, appealing young woman. When she came back with his order, he halfway blurted out, "You're new here, ain't you?"

"Yes," she said, "I'm DeLois, what's your name?"

"I'm Rex. I come in here all the time."

"Rex, that's an interesting name, I don't think I've ever known a Rex."

"So have you always lived in Modesto?" asked Rex.

"Heavens no," she replied. "I've only been in Modesto for less than a week."

"Really? Where are you from?"

"I'm from Golden City, Missouri."

"Where's Golden City?"

"Oh, it's in the western part of Missouri, not far from Greenfield, if you've ever heard of that."

Rex's confidence began to build. He had been fooled by this young woman's speech and dress. He had taken her for a California native.

"You don't talk like a Missourian," Rex offered.

"What do I talk like?"

"Well, I thought you was borned here," said Rex.

"Borned here?" DeLois laughed.

"Born here," Rex corrected himself.

The two "immigrants" found an instant rapport. In a few minutes they figured out that they had grown up only eighty miles from each other, DeLois in western Missouri and Rex in eastern Oklahoma. Rex chose his words carefully after she had corrected his English. It wasn't that Rex didn't recognize proper grammar, for the most part, just that most people he associated with talked like him. Before Rex left, he suggested that perhaps they could meet someplace socially and get to know each other better. DeLois accepted his invitation and the next day a whirlwind romance began.

DeLois had been born on her father, Clinton Bowles', farm and had lost her mother at age three. Clinton and Da-

Rex & DeLois Tanner's Wedding Day 1937

sha, DeLois' mother, had eleven children, seven boys and four girls. Clinton remarried not long after his wife's untimely death, to one of his older daughter's girlfriends. The girl was in her late teens, Clinton in his mid-forties. The age discrepancy was a bit of an embarrassment to some of the family members, even in rural nineteen-twenty Missouri, but Clinton was devoted and respectful to his new wife, who bore him three additional children.

DeLois moved to town to live with one of her sisters when she began high school and upon graduating, announced she wanted to move to California. Clinton agreed to provide the money for her to go and asked her brother Orval to take her. Orval had expressed interest in joining his two older brothers Archie and Everett, who had moved to California previously and seemed to be doing well. Orval was a powerfully built young man with a sparkling sense of humor and an uncommon work ethic. Most men, when sizing him up, immediately gave him a wide berth. He had brought DeLois to California and had taken her up the San Joaquin Valley to various cities. Truth be known, Orval wanted to see some of Northern California before he committed to living near his brothers in the Riverside/San Bernadino area of Southern California.

DeLois liked Modesto and said she'd like to try living there. She was nineteen. Orval found her a nice room with a good family in the downtown area and after she secured the job at the coffee shop, he left for the Riverside area.

Rex and DeLois were inseparable from the beginning and when it became obvious that neither one was going to be looking for anyone else, they decided to get married. Their courtship lasted three months.

Rex was not intimidated by DeLois's education and self-confidence, but he began to try to improve his grammar and lose his Oklahoma brogue. That didn't exactly endear him to his casual friends and fellow workers in the orchards,

Orval Bowles (circa 1937)

so he began to speak one way when he was with them and another when he was with her. Clearly, his self-image and level of sophistication were noticeably elevated from his association with her.

Orval, meanwhile, learned of the marriage and considered it an affront to his protective responsibility. He drove straight away to Modesto with the intention of getting to the bottom of what was happening and putting it to an end. When Orval found the two lovers, he immediately got out of his car and confronted Rex.

"Are you the Okie bastard that thinks he just married my sister?" Orval yelled.

"I reckon I'm the Okie bastard that's in love with my wife, who may happen to be your sister," Rex returned.

"What kind of bullshit do you call that?" asked Orval. "No one even told anyone in our family."

"Well, after meetin' you," replied Rex, "I'm thinkin' maybe that was a good thing."

Orval looked at Rex long and hard for several moments and when Rex's expression didn't show any emotion, he broke out laughing.

"I'm Rex."

"I figured that," replied Orval.

"Let's go have some dinner and git to know each other," suggested Rex.

"I'm starving," said Orval, as though he'd known Rex his whole life.

Orval had made no plans for what he intended to do after he'd confronted Rex. They invited him to stay with them and sleep on the couch of the small one bedroom house they had rented. Rex went back to the ice factory and Orval found some work during the foggy winter. Orval actually was a farmer and had vast knowledge and skills that allowed him to find work when others could not. He stayed through the summer and amazed locals with the amount of fruit he could pick, sometimes making more than twenty dollars a day.

On one job Orval took the long ladder the rancher's son was using to pick low hanging fruit, while the boy was relieving himself back in the orchard. When the son returned and his ladder was gone, he began looking for it and found Orval on the top rung, high in a heavily laden peach tree.

"Daddy gave me that ladder," the boy hollered up at Orval. "I'm takin' it back."

"You touch that ladder, boy, and you'll be pickin' these peaches with your elbows," hollered back Orval.

"I'm gonna go tell Daddy," whined the boy. "That's my ladder."

"You go tell 'Daddy' that Orval Bowles is pickin' a hundred boxes of peaches today and if he wants to wait a week for your sorry ass to pick 'em, they're gonna rot in the box 'fore they get to market. In the meantime, get your God damn hands off MY ladder."

The boy reluctantly picked up Orval's original ladder and walked back to the tree he'd been working on. "Daddy" never showed and Orval picked a record number of lugs over the next few days, ensuring the farmer's harvest before any fruit went bad.

Rex, meanwhile, had found a job working with Clarace's husband, DeForest Wood, who had moved to Modesto from Claremore a couple of years earlier. De had gone to college for a couple of years in Oklahoma to study engineering and had established himself at a local plumbing company as a foreman. He secured a job for Rex as a laborer, digging trenches and assisting the plumbers with the heavy cast iron and lead components required to build plumbing systems. Rex learned quickly. He was a married man now and instinctively knew that his previous endeavors were not going to be substantial enough to properly fund and sustain a family at the level for which he and DeLois were planning.

In two or three years Rex had become a decent plumber and was making enough money for DeLois and him to live comfortably. They bought a nineteen thirty-seven Plymouth and moved to a larger one-bedroom house. Their first child, a boy, was born in January of nineteen forty. Orval had gone back south after that first summer. By nineteen fifty Orval had established himself as one of Riverside, California's most successful turkey farmers. He and Rex remained close friends until Orval died in nineteen eighty-seven.

In nineteen forty-one, on December 7, Japan bombed Pearl Harbor.

The Girl From Missouri

She was young and pretty
When she left Golden City
In the Spring of nineteen thirty-six
A regular heart breaker
She asked her pa to stake her
The money for a California trip

Her daddy told her brother
This girl has lost her mother
And I've got seven sons that look like you
And I would be a liar
To say I could deny her
Anything she'd ever want to do

Hear the banjo ring across the wide Missouri
Lay the bow across the fiddle too
All the boys you used to know
Back in Joplin and St Joe
Sure are gonna miss the sight of you

And so her brother took her
And she was such a looker
She broke a thousand hearts along the way
She wished 'em all her best though
'til she landed in Modesto
Looked around and said I think I'll stay

Ol' Orval headed south
A cigar in his mouth
To make his name and fortune in the sun
He said don't worry Sis
If anything's amiss

You can count on me to come back on the run

Hear the banjo ring across the wide Missouri
Lay the bow across the fiddle too
All the boys you used to know
Back in Joplin and St Joe
Sure are gonna miss the sight of you

She was waitin' tables
At a coffee shop called 'Mabel's'
When a young peach picker walked in through the door
He was fresh from Oklahoma
Nearly went into a coma
When she smiled and said "I get off work at four"

It was a different world then
They courted in a whirlwind
Three months later they were man and wife
Ol' Orval got the word by wire
His angry eyes were filled with fire
He went back north to take that Okie's life

Hear the banjo ring across the wide Missouri
Lay the bow across the fiddle too
All the boys you used to know
Back in Joplin and St Joe
Sure are gonna miss the sight of you

Now Orval was a farmer's son
He'd never lost to anyone
Men feared him for the muscle in his arm
But the Okie boy was quick and smart

He said "you'll never make us part"
He stood his ground and whipped him with his charm

So Orval didn't stay too long
He wished them luck and then moved on
Sometimes it doesn't pay to voice your fears
They smiled at him and said goodbye
A tear was in my mother's eye
And she lived with my old man mor'n fifty years

Hear the banjo ring across the wide Missouri
Lay the bow across the fiddle too
I'm so glad you didn't go
Back to Joplin or St Joe
And I just want to say I still love you

Words & Music by Gary Rex Tanner

Songs from this book can be heard at
www.oklahomagamblinman.com

To hear songs written & performed by Gary Rex Tanner
Please visit www.garyrextanner.com

21

The Shipyard

Shortly after World War II began, notices were posted around Modesto that welding classes were being held at Modesto Junior College. After successful completion, a certification would be given to enable successful applicants to work in the Bay Area Shipyards. Rex signed up and attended welding classes five times a week for four hours a night, after work, for six months. Rex had done some welding as a boy, working at the junkyard and again periodically working locally as a plumber. Rex passed his certification test easily and he and DeLois moved to Berkeley, California, and Rex got a job as a welder at Kaiser's Richmond Shipyard. The shipyard was a world unto itself: cranes and cables going everywhere, men scurrying about, welding torches flashing from every direction and location. On the first day of orientation Rex was introduced to a man named Conn. The noise of the yard made it impossible for

“Conn” & “Tex” 1943

Rex to make out his first name and he simply said, "Glad to meet you, Conn."

Conn couldn't hear Rex's name correctly either and replied, "Glad to meet you, too, Tex."

So Conn and Tex became a welding team. Conn was a former professional hockey player and had the flare and aggressive nature one might expect. Rex was cool and fearless and Conn once said about Rex, "Tex throws a railroad tie over the toilet seat when he takes a shit, so his balls don't touch the water."

The two new friends carpooled in Rex's '37 Plymouth. Rex had never experienced the heavy traffic that surrounded the shipyard, and they made a game out of trying to get past as many slow moving vehicles as they could, both going to and coming from work.

"How's she look off starboard, Conn?" Rex would ask.

"Take 'er on the right, Tex," Conn would reply.

They would cut through traffic, narrowly missing other cars and trucks, with people honking and giving them the finger and Conn climbing halfway out the window, yelling back obscenities. It didn't escape Rex's memory that had he made a different choice a few years earlier, he might have done similar driving had he joined Bernie and the gamblers the last time he saw them in Claremore. Near the end of their second year at the shipyard, their foreman, a gentleman of Italian descent, asked for volunteers to make the final welds on the crow's nest of the ship they were building, some 70 feet above the deck. No one volunteered and the supervisor looked directly at Rex and said, "How about you, Tanner? You aren't afraid of heights, are you?"

"I don't scare," replied Rex. "I ain't scared of nothin'…I ain't never been scared of nothin'."

"Then why don't you get your welding rig together and I'll find someone to help you."

"I'll go," answered Conn. "Me 'n' Tex are a team; where he goes I go."

"Oh, that's good," said the supervisor. "The rest of you guys get back to what you were doing."

Rex and Conn got their equipment in order and followed their supervisor up the ladder to the crow's nest, where a platform had been placed for them to stand on while the welds were made. Once at the top, their boss instructed them as to what he wanted and then descended the ladder. When the two welders were both in place and the equipment was ready, Rex stepped out onto the platform. Immediately the platform collapsed and Rex fell, almost certainly to his death. After falling about 25 feet, Rex saw a cable that was being used to stabilize an adjacent structure, and he reached for it and held on for dear life. The cable sagged about 20-30 feet, almost completely stopping Rex's fall and then, when all of the slack had been used, it suddenly sprang back upwards from the tension, out of Rex's grasp, dropping him the final 20-25 feet to the deck of the ship. Rex landed on his right side. The same arm that had been broken in the football game in Claremore took the brunt of the fall. Rex lay there, stunned but still conscious, with the wind knocked out of him, as workers from every direction came to his aid. Conn was coming down the ladder that led to the crow's nest like a mama bear protecting one of her cubs. By the time Conn got to the deck, there was a large circle of men around Rex, and Conn pushed through them to get to his friend. At about the same time the ship's medics had arrived and were beginning to attend to Rex, trying to determine the extent of his injuries.

"Jesus Christ!" yelled Conn. "Are you all right, Tex?"

"I don't know, Conn, I think my arm might be broke and I'm havin' trouble catchin' my breath."

"You Dago son of a bitch," screamed Conn as he caught sight of the supervisor who had sent them to do the welds on the crow's nest, "you knew that platform wasn't connected and you sent Tex up there 'cause you're a God damn fascist and now we know you're a saboteur."

"You're crazy," replied the supervisor. "My family has lived in America for three generations. We don't even know anybody in Italy."

"You're a lyin' son of a bitch," raged Conn, by now being held back by several coworkers.

"Look, asshole," replied the Italian, "you say one more word like that and you'll be out on the street looking for a job."

"I don't give a shit; me 'n' Tex can find a job anyplace."

Now Rex was on his feet and being led carefully to the infirmary. No one was working, just talking about what they had just witnessed: a man falling 70 feet and getting up and walking away. No one had seen Rex grab the cable and believed they had just seen somewhat of a miracle. Conn followed the medics and Rex to the infirmary as the crowd dispersed and the men returned to their jobs. The supervisor was taken upstairs to give a report of the details of what had happened. Rex and Conn were given the rest of the day off and went home. Rex was advised to stay home, with pay, for as many days as he felt necessary, until he was ready to work. Rex was badly bruised but had no broken bones or ligament damage. He returned to work the third day. Conn was transferred to another ship, far away from the supervisor he had confronted. Rex wasn't comfortable with the new partner he'd been assigned to, and the supervisor began criticizing everything he worked on. Conn was transferred to the swing shift, so the camaraderie of the drive back and forth to work was gone, too. After about a week, Rex went to the personnel office and told them he was quitting.

"You'll be drafted within a month," he was told.

"I'll deal with that when it happens," replied Rex as

he was given his final paycheck and departed.

He sought out Conn, told him of his plans to return to Modesto and said goodbye. Conn cried when they parted, and the two friends never heard from each other again.

Rex did receive his draft notice in a few weeks. He was 31 years old, with one child and another on the way. DeLois petitioned the draft board for a deferment so he could be there for the birth of the new baby, and he was given a six-month deferment. Before the extension was completed, the war was over and he was not further notified.

During the couple of days that Rex was convalescing from the crow's nest accident, there was a knock at the front door.

"Rex, there's someone to see you," called out DeLois, who had answered the door.

Rex walked from the kitchen into the living room, and there stood Kilmer.

"Hey cousin," greeted Kilmer, "I hears yore down there at the ship yards makin' boats."

"Kilmer!" Rex exclaimed. "Has it been ten years or did you break out of the pen?"

"Reckon it's been eleven years, countin' the time in Tulsa."

"Are you gonna be livin' here now?" asked Rex.

"Naw, I just come by to see how you was doin'…I'm goin' back to Oklahoma in a few days."

"What are you gonna do?" asked Rex.

"Well, I know this is gonna sound funny, but I'm travelin' with this tent revival and they pay me to git up and tell folks about my life and testify for the Lord. I reckon I'll stay with 'em for a while, 'til I can figure out what I want to do with the rest of my life."

"You ain't shittin' me, are you, cousin?"

"Naw, Rex, not this time. That's the God's honest truth."

While the two cousins were catching up, Kilmer gazed over Rex's shoulder and saw the view of the bay. He walked to the window and gazed across the water to Alcatraz. Kilmer had met several people at Leavenworth that had been transferred to "The Rock."

"I'll tell you one thing, cousin," Kilmer said, "I ain't ever goin' back to prison. It's a tough ol' row to hoe. Them ol' boys over there don't ever have a nice day."

As Kilmer spoke, tears began to stream down his cheek, making Rex extremely uncomfortable. Rex could not remember ever crying himself and seeing Kilmer react emotionally took him aback. Rex realized at this moment that this was not the Kilmer he had known growing up in Oklahoma and when he would next see him again, seven years later, Kilmer would be traveling with another tent revival, through Modesto this time, "featured" as a "guest speaker" who testified about how God had led him from his evil ways back into the fold.

When Rex made his decision to return to Modesto, he went over to San Francisco to see Frank and tell him of his plans. Arriving at Frank's apartment early on a Saturday afternoon, he found Ruby alone. She advised him that Frank had gone a few blocks down the street to a neighborhood bar. Rex followed Ruby's directions and came to a bar in the middle of the block where a small group of people were milling around outside, one of them dressed as what Rex took to be a bartender.

"What's goin' on?" Rex said to no one in particular.

"There's a crazy son of a bitch with a knife in there, threatening to cut people up," said the bartender.

"Why's he wanna do that?" Rex asked.

"Beats the shit out of me," answered the bartender. "We were just having a normal conversation and he gits up and walks behind the bar and shows me a knife that you could use to skin a deer."

"What's he look like?" asked Rex.

"He's kinda skinny, with thin hair and mean lookin' eyes."

"Maybe I'll go in and see if I can talk with 'im," said Rex.

"You better just wait here, buddy…we already called the cops. I'd say he's for sure dangerous."

"I think I'll go in and just take a look," replied Rex. "I'll run back out the door if he gits after me."

"You're takin' a big risk, there fella," warned the bartender. "He's probably gonna kill somebody before the day's over."

Rex pushed through the swinging doors and saw the man at the far end of the bar staring at him.

"Hey Frank," Rex greeted, proceeding to where Frank sat.

"Rex," replied his brother Frank.

"What's all the rhubarb about?" asked Rex.

Frank did his best to suppress the smile that was trying to capture his lips. "Why, that dumb-ass bartender and a couple of them other pricks was runnin' down the Okies and I heard enough of it and walked back behind the bar and introduced them to Mr. Barlow."

"Shit, Frank, what do you care what they say about Okies? Hell-fahr, if they thought you was one, they'd have prob'ly not said anything a'tall. The last thing you need is to git in another knife fight."

"Them assholes ain't gonna fight no one; they're all mouth…they don't know shit from apple butter, especially about Okies--or much of anything else."

"Well, they say they called the cops. I reckon we better git on out that back door 'fore they git here," offered Rex.

"Hell, the cops out here ain't like them cops back home. They turn on the siren a mile or two 'fore they git to where they're goin', hopin' whoever they're comin' after already left."

"Well, then we got plenty of time to git out of here 'fore they git here," reasoned Rex.

While Frank was discussing the situation with his brother, he had casually walked behind the bar, prepared himself a double martini and was proceeding to ingest its contents.

"They prob'ly didn't think I was an Okie 'cause I drink martinis," Frank speculated.

"Here, pour me a double shot of that Seagram's Seven," instructed Rex, pushing a nearby shot glass toward his brother. "If we're gonna wait here for the law, I might as well have a couple of free drinks."

"We ain't gonna wait," corrected Frank. "We just ain't in a hurry to go, that's all. We ain't goin' out the back door, neither. Come on, let's go."

With that, Frank finished his drink, walked from behind the bar and headed to the front door with Rex following. Out on the street, Frank surveyed the assembled crowd, which had doubled by now, and spoke to no one in particular. "Next week, when I come in here, I'll expect all you assholes to show some respect for people less fortunate than you are and keep your God damn mouths shut if you cain't say somethin' good about anyone. I will say one thing, though, the martinis here ain't half bad, even if you have to make'em yourself…I left a dollar and a half on the bar to pay for the one I made for myself and the double shot of whiskey my brother drank."

Frank and Rex slowly sauntered up the street to Frank's apartment. The crowd slowly dispersed, most returning to the bar. Half an hour later the brothers, safely inside Frank and Ruby's apartment, heard sirens heading in the direction of the bar.

Frank & Ruby Tanner (circa 1943)

22

Return To Modesto

Rex and DeLois returned to Modesto, and the following two years passed very quickly. The war ended and Rex found employment at a plumbing company that was expanding rapidly with the improved economy. Their second child, another boy, was born. They sold the '37 Plymouth and ordered a new nineteen forty-six Chevrolet four-door sedan from the factory for eight hundred dollars, cash. They were able to save enough money to put down on a modest eight hundred square foot, two bedroom house on the fringe of a nice neighborhood. Across the street and a couple of doors down was a gas station grocery store, which was common in that era, facing a well traveled thoroughfare. The house was purchased from a veterinarian, Dr. Stieger, who lived around the corner and whose barn and horse corral adjoined the rear of their new property. Life was good. Rex worked long hours, and they quickly paid for the new house and were able to save some money.

Rex, being the gambler he was, was a bit loose with his money, whereas DeLois was practical, prudent and careful with the money Rex earned. Rex gave DeLois his paycheck every Friday and never asked her to return any of it to cover whatever expenses he might encounter. Rex, similar to Frank's Barlow, always had a billfold full of money that no one ever saw.

Rex loved his two boys and unlike his father, Leonard, spent most of his free time with them and their mother. Rex was beginning to realize he had a bright future ahead of him, if he played his cards right.

Frank and Ruby moved from the bay area to Modesto, and Frank soon became a successful cement contractor.

On the west side of Modesto, out Shiloh Road, there was a dance hall that was popular with young working couples in nineteen forty-six. Rex and DeLois met two other couples there one Friday night for a respite from the busy schedule they had been keeping. Everyone was having a wonderful time and near the end of the evening, as they were leaving, Rex excused himself to use the restroom. When he came out, he saw DeLois and the other couples standing near the snack bar waiting for him.

"Did you order some coffee?" Rex inquired.

"We tried to," said DeLois, "but no one would wait on us."

Rex turned and walked up to the snack bar counter and asked for service. "Can we git six cups of coffee?" he said, and a young woman whose back was to him turned around and began filling six cups of coffee for him. Rex hardly noticed the two large men standing near their entourage and began distributing the coffee to his companions.

When he glanced in the direction of the men, one of them said, "It must be nice to know someone, so you can get service around here."

The men were two twenty-something Portuguese dairy farmers, very large in stature and somewhat menacing in nature.

"Naw, I'm just like you," answered Rex. "I don't know anyone here. I just happened to git that gal's attention and she got our coffee."

"You ain't like us," replied the dairy farmer. "We're Portagees and you're a bunch of low-life Okies."

Rex bristled but retained his composure. The one Portagee that was doing the talking was obviously inebriated. His brother, standing beside him with his hand inside his topcoat pocket, kept a poker face and carefully monitored the ensuing conversation. Rex was glad his coffee wasn't very hot and he drank it quickly while listening to the man berating him and his friends.

"I think this must be the most Okies I've ever seen in one place at one time," the Portagee continued. "How'd a little shit-ass like you get a gal like her?" he said with a grin, nodding at DeLois.

By now Rex had finished his coffee and was wrapping his fingers around the very thick, heavy ceramic cup that was now empty. As the man passed a sneering glance toward his brother for support, Rex threw a roundhouse punch, connecting near the temple of the big man's head with the coffee cup. The man slowly dropped to his knees, holding his head, and Rex wound up like a baseball pitcher with a full windup and threw the cup point blank at the man's head. The cup hit the top of his head and ricocheted out into the dispersing crowd, and Rex turned to complete his intended mission of kicking the poker-faced brother in the groin, when suddenly he felt someone pin his arms to his side from behind. An off-duty deputy sheriff who had been hired by the dance promoter for security had been standing nearby and instinctively took the initiative to try to stop the altercation.

The poker-faced man stepped forward with a blackjack that he had been holding inside his topcoat pocket and caught Rex on the bridge of the nose, breaking his nose for the third time. Rex bent forward in pain, trying to avoid the following blows, and the poker-face literally beat the off-duty deputy sheriff unconscious. The sheriff had let go of Rex after the first blackjack blow hit him.

Rex grabbed DeLois and the other two women and fled through the crowd of stampeding Okies, Portagees and native Californians. The two men that had accompanied Rex and DeLois, with their wives, anticipating a fight, had run outside to their cars to secure tire irons, leaving the women inside unprotected. The three couples left the dance hall parking lot with tires screeching, not waiting to see if the deputy was being attended to, and saw the two dairy farmers slowly limping to their car. Rex woke up the next morning with a badly broken nose and two black eyes. The poker-faced brother had found his mark well. Someone called to say that the deputy had been hospitalized, and Rex called Doc Stieger and went next door to have him set his nose. There was no use to go to a regular doctor. Doc Stieger told him after you break your nose three or four times, there's only so much you can do with it.

Rex went to work Monday morning and sometime shortly after lunch, a police car pulled up on the job on which Rex was working and two officers approached him and said, "We're looking for Rex Tanner."

"That's me," said Rex. "What's the trouble?"

"You're under arrest for assault and battery on a law enforcement officer," one policeman said. "We're here to take you in."

"Shit, fellas," responded Rex, "I never assaulted no police officer."

"It's nothing to do with us," the policeman said. "We're just here to take you in."

The policemen allowed Rex to pick up his tools and make arrangements with the plumbers with whom he was working to keep them safe for him. The policemen handcuffed him and drove him to the police station.

"We got Rex Tanner here," one of the policemen announced as they came into the station.

"Put him in a holding cell until we can see if he can make bail," said the person that seemed to be in charge.

The policemen led Rex back to the holding cell and opened it. As Rex entered the cell, he was startled to see that the two men already inside were the two brothers whom he had had the altercation with two days earlier. Rex's instincts were to stay calm and to try to protect himself as much as possible. Quickly sizing up the situation, he walked briskly to the rear corner and turned facing the brothers, who were standing near the entrance to the cell, and wedged himself into the corner with his hands grasping the cell bars above his head. His only possible defense, he reasoned, was to try to keep them off him with kicks, with which he was quite skillful.

The officers walked back into the area from whence they had come, leaving Rex alone in the cell with the two brothers. The brother with the big mouth and bruised head slowly approached Rex, peering curiously at him from head to toe.

"Are you the man that knocked me down at the dance the other night?" he asked.

"Reckon maybe I am," said Rex cautiously.

"How much you weigh, fella?"

"About a hundred and sixty pounds," Rex answered

"No shit," the man said. "I'm gonna tell you something, mister, I get in a fight almost every weekend and you're the first son of a bitch that ever knocked me down. I can't believe a man your size could hit as hard as you hit me."

Rex realized at this point that neither brother knew he had hit him with the coffee cup.

"So I got this big knot on the top of my head," the mouthy brother continued, "What...did you kick me after you knocked me down?"

"Naw, I would've but somebody grabbed me from behind and your partner there hit me in the nose with a blackjack."

"Aw shit," said the man, "he probably shouldn't have done that. Hell, it was a good fight and you knocked me down fair and square. I tell you what…you got a pair of balls takin' a shot at a man my size…I got to give you credit."

"Yeah," said Rex, remembering what Conn had said about him a couple of years earlier, "whenever I go to take a shit, my balls touch the water."

The man looked at Rex incredulously and then suddenly burst out laughing. The poker-faced brother couldn't keep a straight face, either, and in a few seconds both brothers were laughing uproariously, with tears streaming down their faces.

In a few minutes an officer came and took Rex from the holding cell. He was released on two hundred-fifty dollars bail and given a court appearance date. A month later he pled guilty to a charge of disturbing the peace and was fined fifty dollars. The brother he had knocked down was fined an equal amount and the poker-faced brother got thirty days in the county jail for assault and battery. Because the deputy was off-duty and working independently for the dance promoters, more serious charges were dropped.

23

The Plumbin' Shop

As the next couple of years rolled by, Rex became increasingly proficient in his trade as a plumber. He had joined the plumbers' union and was certified as a journeyman plumber, and he began to consider opening his own company. His ambitions were modest; he thought perhaps he'd just buy a truck and work for people he knew around the neighborhood and family and friends. The economy was robust in California after the war, and tradesmen were in great demand.

An old German couple, the Mechs, owned and operated a gas station grocery store across the street from Rex and DeLois's home, two houses south, facing a two lane thoroughfare, Yosemite Boulevard. The old man was in his eighties, an avid fisherman, and Rex had gone fishing with him a few times and they had become friends. Mr. Mech suggested to Rex that he lease the store from his son, close

the gas pumps, fence the yard and try a more ambitious business approach. Rex slowly began to see Mr. Mech's vision, and after studying for the California State Plumbing Contractor's license examination for several months, Rex went to Sacramento and passed the examination, receiving his State Contractor's License--no small feat for someone not having completed the third grade.

Passing the exam gave Rex a burst of self confidence and in nineteen forty-eight, he opened his business at 719 Yosemite Boulevard, Modesto, California. Whatever modest goals Rex may have had were quickly replaced by the onslaught of business that came to him through his natural business skills, winning personality, ambition and natural work ethic. In nineteen fifty, Rex took as payment for an eighteen hundred dollar debt a very low mileage nineteen forty-eight Cadillac Fleetwood sedan that had been made for Chiang Kai-shek but had not been delivered due to his ouster as the leader of China. Rex took his family and drove to Claremore in the '48 Cadillac later that year, looking up old friends and acquaintances, mainly to let them know he had found success. He never returned, commenting that when he drove out of town that last time, he started at the east end of the main street and kept the accelerator on the floor until he exited the west end of the town and never looked back.

By nineteen fifty-one, Rex and Morris owned and operated twenty-five plumbing vehicles and had a workforce and staff of forty employees.

Being a union plumber, Rex preferred to operate as a union business. In nineteen fifty-three the local plumber's union demanded an unprecedented wage increase to three dollars an hour. Rex, being a member of the local Associated Plumbing Contractors, along with the other members, refused to comply. The union immediately went on strike. Ironically, Rex had government contracts for plumbing several schools, which included completion dates and daily

Morris & Sue Tanner

penalties for non-compliance. As the strike continued and the dates grew nearer, Rex consulted an attorney for advice and was told he could sign an agreement to pay the asked-for wages independently of the Associated Plumbing Contractors and resume work. Otherwise, he was told, he would have to accept the penalties imposed upon him by the signed government contracts. Rex decided to survive in business, he must sign the agreement, which he did and resumed work.

Within a few days he was sued by the Associated Plumbing Contractors for one hundred and seventy thousand dollars for breaking ranks, contrary to his signed agreement as an active member.

The lawsuit caught the fancy of a reporter for the Modesto Bee, who wrote a front page article sympathetic to the union and mocking the lawsuit. Since in nineteen fifty-three trade unions had much public support, Rex was viewed by many as a sympathetic advocate of working tradesmen.

Three days later, at a family birthday party, the phone rang and a voice at the other end advised Rex that his plumbing shop was on fire. Rex, Frank, their younger brother Charlie and two or three brothers-in-law ran to the Cadillac, which was parked at the curb outside. With tires screeching as the car made a U-turn, Leonard ran alongside the car trying to get in. In the rush someone slammed the door shut, leaving Leonard cursing in the middle of the street as the Cadillac roared into the night, in the direction of the fire. The party was only a five-minute drive from the plumbing shop and when Rex and the other family members arrived, they were only a couple of minutes behind the fire department vehicles. Rex abruptly stopped the Cadillac in the parking area in front of the shop and ran to the front door, as the others ran to the back yard and began driving trucks, some with tires afire, out of the parking area. The rear of the old grocery building was completely engulfed in flames as

Rex kicked in the glass panel of the front door before any fireman could stop him and ran to the filing cabinet in the front office that contained his folders of accounts receivable. Rex quickly grabbed the files, turned around, ran back out the door he had just kicked in and in a matter of seconds the entire office was shooting flames sixty feet into the air. Later, Rex would joke that he took the risk because he was afraid he couldn't remember who owed him money. Rex and the other men stayed through the night and when it was all done, the entire shop and office had burned to the ground. Although only three trucks were lost, thanks to the efforts of the brothers and brothers-in-law, as well as the firemen, the total loss was estimated at eighty-thousand dollars. Unfortunately, Rex had allowed most of his fire insurance policies to lapse, planning to increase them, but not doing so due to the busy work schedule he had been keeping.

Regardless, every job was manned the day after the fire and all the completion dates were met, and in a few weeks the Associated Plumbing Contractors capitulated and the plumber's union prevailed. Within a few days the FBI came to Rex and advised him that they were considering the fire as an act of arson and that they were investigating the events that had led up to the fire. From that day on, Rex kept a loaded .38 revolver in the glove compartment of his Cadillac, a Springfield Armory 1911, .45 semi-automatic in his office and another in the nightstand next to his bed at home. A few months later an FBI agent met with Rex and gave him four names of whom the FBI considered as the perpetrators of having the arson done and the name of the man they suspected of actually starting the fire. No hard evidence was ever forthcoming, and it took Rex a dozen years to overcome the financial loss caused by the fire.

THE MODESTO BEE

and News-Herald

VOL. 76—NO. 165 ★ Founded 1884 MODESTO, CALIFORNIA, SATURDAY, JULY 11, 1953 42 PAGES Phone 2-6461

$170,000 Is Asked In Suit Over Labor Pact

Continued from Page 1

in Berkeley attending the quarterly meeting of the Northern California group.

Discuss Strike

They are expected to devote a good deal of time to the strike situation.

In another development, a spokesman for the local employers says Cloward has threatened to picket combination shops, those employing both sheet metal workers and plumbers.

The sheet metal contractors are negotiating with Local 495 for a new contract, offering 10 cents an hour to $2.72½ and 1¼ cents to the welfare fund, a total of 7½ cents. The union is asking $3 per hour and a 10 cents per hour welfare payment.

No picketing has been reported, however.

In San Francisco the week old strike of 1,000 AFL plumbers in San Francisco, Marin, Sonoma and Mendocino Counties has ended.

Win Demands

Workers won their demands for a 15 cents per hour increase, including welfare benefits.

However, 2,500 other AFL plumbers are still on strike in 11 cities from Bakersfield to Redding.

Other news on the strike front:

Settlement of a coastwide strike is in sight involving 1,500 AFL machinists at 60 shipyards. Machinists must okeh the formula reached yesterday.

Still No Progress

A "desperation" meeting of the Associated General Contractors and the AFL laborers' union ended with no progress reported.

Last local reports were the situation is "hopeless."

The Associated Farmers warned members a strike in the huge fruit and vegetable canning industry is imminent. There is a wage dispute between cannery workers and the California Processors and Growers.

Plumbing Group Sue Member In Contract Row

The local labor dispute between plumbers and employers over a new contract burst in another direction yesterday, as the Associated Plumbing Contractors of Stanislaus and Merced Counties sued one of its members for $170,000.

In a civil action filed in the superior court here the association charges Rex Tanner, plumbing contractor at 719 Yosemite Boulevard, with negotiating an interim contract after he assigned his bargaining powers to another agency.

Tanner assertedly signed a pact with Local 437, American Federation of Labor. R. L. Cloward, business agent, says the agreement calls for 25 cents per hour and higher welfare fund payments.

Plumbers were demanding 12½ cents in wages and a 2½ cents per hour increase in welfare over the $3 per hour and 7½ cents in welfare they are receiving. The best employer offer, made so far—10 cents in wages—has been withdrawn.

17 Join In Suit

Seventeen members of the association are joining in the suit against Tanner, alleging they authorized the Northern California Conference of Plumbing and Heating Contractors to represent their group in negotiations with the union.

It alleges further that Tanner joined the association July 2nd (Thursday) with full knowledge of its organization and plans but 48 hours later signed an agreement with the union.

Today Archie Gray, member of the negotiating committee, Harold Newman and Fred Hill, directors of the association, are

Continued on Page 2, Col. 7

THE MODESTO BEE

and News-Herald

VOL. 76—NO. 170 ★ Founded 1884 MODESTO, CALIFORNIA, FRIDAY, JULY 17, 1953 20 PAGES Phone 3-6461 PRICE: Ten Cents Per Copy $1.50 Monthly By Carrier

AP Wirephoto

$45,000 Plumbing Shop Fire May Be Incendiary

Arson may be the cause of a $45,000 fire which burned to the ground the Rex A. Tanner plumbing works at 719 Yosemite Boulevard about 10:30 o'clock last night.

County Fire Warden O. S. Ball, who inspected the fire carefully this afternoon, said "it could be and it couldn't be. We're looking carefully."

Ball hopes to question a person who is said to have turned in an early alarm after trying unsuccessfully to put out the fire himself.

Officials now are investigating the blaze which in their words "was just too much fire at one time."

Punctuated by bursting oil tanks which shook the ground and threw yellow sheets

See photos on Page 4

of flame in a near Fourth of July display, the fire gutted the building and left only part of a sagging roof with a clock stopped at 10:32 PM.

Fireman Reports Blaze

The fire was reported to Empire Firehouse No. 2 by Leroy Burke, an assistant at the fire station, who was returning with a friend from a swim. It dispatched two trucks, Empire No. 1 sent another truck, and two trucks from the county joined them.

The plumbing works was owned by Tanner and his brother, Morris J. Tanner, who leased the property and building.

Tanner says he has only about $7,000 insurance on the estimated loss. The building was insured.

the property and building.

Tanner says he has only about $7,000 insurance on the estimated loss. The building was insured.

The building is owned by the estate of Moser, Adams and Warnock. Andy Moser is executor. He placed the value of the building at only $10,000 to $12,000 and said insurance was less than that amount.

Tanner was at a party at the home of his mother, Mrs. A. L. Tanner of 606 Fifteenth Street, when neighbors called him about 10:45 PM. He could see the flames on his way over.

Equipment Is Lost

Tanner said he managed to save his books and files, including ledgers and accounts receivable. In addition, spectators helped volunteer firemen wheel three of four service trucks out of the blaze, but the other truck plus mounds of furnaces, toilets, heaters, coolers and other plumbing supplies appear to be a total loss.

Firemen got the situation under control about 12:30 AM today. At that time crews of the Pacific Telephone and Telegraph Company went to work to restore service to some 1,000 homes in the area, whose connections were cut off when cables near the building were destroyed in the fire.

The telephone company said today 30 per cent service was restored by 10 AM and all phones should be in operation by 4 PM. Eight splicing crews worked during the night.

Ball, his assistant, Les Baker, sheriff's deputies and the California Highway Patrol took part in the fire fighting.

The fire is believed to have started within a wire enclosure on the east side of the building.

To the west of the building is a mound of 30,000 wooden lugs. Flames jumped to the back fence but did not touch the boxes.

CLOCK TELLS STORY—The hands of the clock, stopped at about 10:32 o'clock last night, show the progress the fire made by that time. It gutted the Rex Tanner Plumbing Company at 719 Yosemite Boulevard, resulting in an estimated $45,000 loss in supplies, plus destruction of the building. Butane tanks exploded and telephone wires were burned out, shutting off service to some 1,000 homes.

TOTAL LOSS—Although volunteer firemen play hoses on the smoldering wreckage, little is left of the plumbing company. To the right is one of four trucks which was pulled out of the fire. Three were in fair condition but the fourth was a total loss. Tires and paint burned on all of them. Spectators helped get them out. See story on Page 1. Bee Photos

Judge Fi
Firm, Aic
For Cavei

McClatchy Newspapers

TURLOCK — Found putting shorings too in a ditch which cave caused the death of Ar kins, 62, of Hilmar, t ton Construction Com its foreman, John Wei were fined $250 each.

Turlock Judicial Judge Harry O. Carls the case in which the representing Wiebe company admitted t tions but argued they tremely minor in nat contended absolute c with the law is "almo sible."

The attorney sug $100 fine would be cited a later accident shorings had three fo to argue the distance shorings was not the safety factor.

Inspector Testif

Testifying as to s tions was Herbert Turlock city inspecto job. Joe Roberts, lab representative of the sion of industrial saf fied the shorings were feet apart instead of the law specified. It erts who signed the charging the firm a with the misdemeanor

Tompkins died Feb of a broken leg and cation of both shou other injuries when sides caved in. Anoth February 3rd buried Arthur, 52, of Turlo his waist. His back wa

The accident occur the Stockton Constru pany was laying th Turlock outfall sewer the sewer farm to Hod

Death Of Tw
Korea Is Laic
AF Sergea

TAEGU, Korea—U of premeditated m tempted murder an have been filed agai force sergeant accus ing two airmen and two others, the 5th said today.

The charges we against Staff Sergea Redmond, Shavertow ing held at the 5th correction center nea

Redmond, alleged began firing a car group of airmen th

Conversely, the fire may have motivated him to greater success and accomplishment. Over the thirty-five years Rex was in the plumbing business, his company was responsible for the plumbing systems of tens of thousands of homes, apartments, businesses and commercial buildings. His company contracted jobs from as far north as Chico, as far south as Bakersfield, east to Lake Tahoe and west to San Jose and the Bay Area.

Rex lived his life simply, never seeking or displaying an appetite for ostentatious wealth. His idea of success, besides having a comfortable home, was having two Cadillacs for him and DeLois and ten or fifteen thousand dollars in cash in his wallet, usually in five hundred and thousand dollar bills. Having his name on a building and on his trucks gave him a sense of pride and accomplishment, and he took responsibility for sharing his success with his family, friends and anyone he felt he could help by giving them employment and teaching them his trade. Scores of employees and family members were influenced over the years by the support and example that Rex gave them to start their own businesses.

Rex had one weakness in business: he was an eternal optimist. When the final tally was in at the end of thirty-five years, it was shown that Rex had written off over a million dollars in bad debts. He was, after all, a gambler, and when he died in 1993 at the age of eighty, he had no debt and his only asset was whatever equity that was in his 1985 Lincoln Town Car. Like the gambler in the famous song, he had…in effect…literally, broken even.

California Pie

My sweet Granny and my grandpa Len
Came to Oklahoma on the western wind
They were just lookin' for a better home
But all they found was an old dust bowl
They had three sons that I knew well
I'll tell y'all about 'em if you sit a spell

Bye bye Oklahoma sky
Save me some of that California pie

Ol' Frank Tanner he was tough as nails
If you stirred him up he was mean as hell
I don't know but it's been said
He once took a knife and left a man dead
It's been so long since he's been gone
He left me here to sing this song

My old man he didn't have much school
But he tried to teach me not to be a fool
Back in Claremore Oklahoma the story's told
He used to make a livin' playin' dominos
Me I was born in the winter time
You can tell everybody I'm doin' fine

Bye bye Oklahoma sky
Save me some of that California pie

Now there's always got to be a joker of course
And I used to call him Uncle Morris
Me and him we used to make the rounds
We've been kicked out of every joint in town
He loved life and he lived so free

But he always took the time to keep an eye on me

Ol' Morris was a dude and a bit of a rogue
And he had just a touch of an Okie brogue
With a pencil thin mustache he wore with style
He cocked his hat with a wink and a smile
Lord it felt like a hammer hit the side of my head
When they told me that my uncle Morris was dead

Bye bye Oklahoma Sky
Save me some of that California pie

Now every summer when I go north
I see the old man and the stories come forth
And though I've heard 'em all a thousand times
They still send chills up and down my spine
And three young heroes are caught in time
And live inside an old man's mind

Bye bye Oklahoma sky
Save me some of that California pie

Words & Music by Gary Rex Tanner

Songs from this book can be heard at
www.oklahomagamblinman.com

To hear songs written & performed by Gary Rex Tanner
Please visit www.garyrextanner.com

Whistle A Sweet Melody

Whistle a sweet melody
Bring back an old memory
When I was a boy I would sing a sad song
You'd whistle in pure harmony
You were a hero to me
All that I wanted to be
A two fisted fighter a buckin' horse rider
Whistle a sweet melody

Whistle a song for my sons
Blue eyed and fair-haired young ones
Tell them your stories and all your tall tales
Just like you did for me once
Teach them a funny old song
God knows they're not children long
And ain't life for livin' and ain't love for givin'
Whistle a sweet melody

Whistle your song like a bird
Sweetest sound ever I've heard
Whistle it sweetly and whistle it slow
Whistle it mellow and low
Share with me your special sound
No finer music I've found
You made the world mine
And you make my sun shine
Whistle a sweet melody

Words & Music by Gary Rex Tanner

When The Goin' Gets Tough

Back on the cotton fields way down south
My granddaddy's daddy lived from hand to mouth
Scrapped for a livin' didn't do much good
Gave all he had and took what he could
Spoke out plain just like a rooster crowin'
When the goin' gets tough...the tough get goin

My old grandpa was a little blind kid
Couldn't see nothin' 'til the age of ten
By then they said that he was much too old for school
No place left to put him but behind a mule
Bust his back stayed straight though his plow was bowin'
When the goin' gets tough...the tough get goin'

When the goin' gets tough
When the goin' gets tough
When the goin' gets tough
When the goin' gets tough
I may sing the blues but I don't know 'em
When the goin' gets tough...the tough get goin'

My old man settled in the west
Left Oklahoma to avoid arrest
Started out pickin' peaches plums and apricots
Got his education at the school of hard knocks
Some people called it pain he just called it growin'
When the goin' gets tough...the tough get goin'

When I was twelve years old I did the work of a man
Now I can make a livin' with these workin' man's hands
When it gets a little hard to keep my family fed
I just reflect on what my grandpa said

Don't you pay no never mind to that cold wind blowin'
When the going gets tough...the tough get goin'

When the goin' gets tough
When the goin' gets tough
When the goin' gets tough
When the goin' gets tough
I may sing the blues but I don't know 'em
When the goin' gets tough...the tough get goin'

Words & Music by Gary Rex Tanner

Songs from this book can be heard at
www.oklahomagamblinman.com

To hear songs written & performed by Gary Rex Tanner
Please visit www.garyrextanner.com

The Plumbin' Shop

In nineteen hundred and forty-eight
Pappy got his plumbin' license from the state
Across the street was a closed up store
That an old German couple couldn't run no more
Pappy went to see 'em and he said guess what
We're gonna open up a plumbin' shop

Pappy put me to work in '49
Threadin' half–inch pipe with a three way die
In 1950 he smiled & said
You're ten years old its time you poured some lead
Must have been late in 51
He taught me how a plumbin' ditch was done

Before I knew it I was twelve years old
Workin' like a man tryin' to make some dough
The shop burned down in '53
Pappy kicked in the door but couldn't save a thing
People felt sorry 'cause they all thought
Pappy'd lost our plumbin' shop

What he told the family was we didn't die
And as sure as he was born on the 4th of July
He built a new building and by summer's end
We were back to pourin' lead again
Me & cousin Warner and my other cousin Scott
Spent the summer stockin' up the brand new shop

We made it through the fifties and the business grew
I learned to drive a truck and how to run a crew
We made a pile of money then we lost it all too
Then we made it all back by nineteen sixty-two

My brother run the office and I run the back
Pappy run the rest from a Cadillac

I got restless and I left one night
Moved to San Diego 'cause the time was right
The Welborn brothers said it won't last long
My mama said that pappy cried when I was gone
Three years later I said guess what
I think I'll open up a plumbin' shop

The years passed by and times were good
I came back to visit anytime i could
Pappy got old and he sold the store
To the Welborn brothers couldn't run it no more
My brother Dave was doin' great
Makin' lots of money sellin' real estate

Then one morning when my kids were half grown
Pappy called me up on the telephone
He said his tools were getting' rusty and he didn't get
How anyone could tolerate retirement
I said I had a place that he could stay
For 10 years he came to work everyday

Pappy bought a Lincoln and he ran a crew
Taught my sons the business like I wanted him to
Took my daughter with him in the summertime
I watched his back and he watched mine
Then when he thought that his work was done
Went back to Modesto where he started from

Pappy's been gone half-a-dozen years

When I think about him gotta choke back tears
I can still remember when he came home late

That cold winter night in 1948
He winked at my mama and he said guess what
We're gonna open up a plumbin' shop

Words & Music by Gary Rex Tanner

Songs from this book can be heard at
www.oklahomagamblinman.com

To hear songs written & performed by Gary Rex Tanner
Please visit www.garyrextanner.com

24

The Final Chapter

Rex slowly awakened and found himself on a long transport vehicle of some kind that was pulling into an incredibly large depot. Most of his fellow travelers remained asleep as he exited the vehicle and slowly made his way through the mass of humanity that was scattered endlessly in every direction. To his left was a line of people of various ages, mostly young, who seemed to be waiting to catch a ride back in the direction from which he had just come. No one spoke, and Rex was confused about who all these people were and what they were doing here. To his right, up on what appeared to be a large hill, some distance from where he was standing, Rex caught sight of what appeared to be a well-lighted city of some kind, flashing colors of light he had never before seen. Rex studied the terrain and saw that winding through the maze of sleeping, half-conscious and confused people was a narrow road that seemed to lead to the lights of the city on the hill.

Rex began to walk toward the lights, reviewing the past few decades and all the things he had learned and experienced. As he walked, he was reminded of the walk from Mexico back to Texas and how it seemed that he might never get there, and it inspired him to keep walking toward the lights. Finally, after what seemed like an extremely long and difficult uphill trek, he saw up ahead a long, high, beautifully crafted wall that encircled the city of lights. The road led up to the wall, which was interrupted by a sentried gate, pearlescent in color, where a white-robed, long-haired gentleman was checking credentials. The line to enter the city was rather short and Rex waited patiently while the white-robed gentleman reviewed and scrutinized the documents of the people before him. When Rex's turn came, he approached the white-robed gentleman with some trepidation, as he realized he didn't have any documents. As the gentleman was about to address him, there was suddenly a disruption of some kind inside the gate, and the gentleman turned and looked back inside the walls to see what was happening.

"Just a moment," the gentleman said, "I've got to help someone inside with a ruling on a technical matter."

The long-haired gentleman left the gate slightly ajar, and through a small opening Rex could see his brother Frank and cousin Kilmer huddling with the person who had just greeted him and going over some details concerning the rules and regulations of whatever they had been doing. Suddenly, the door swung open a bit more widely and from around the back of the wall a voice said, "Rex, walk through the gate and take a hard left."

Rex didn't hesitate. He recognized the voice and when he followed the ominous instructions, he was not surprised to be standing in front of his brother Morris.

"Come on, let's git away from this gate and I'll tell you what's going on," said Morris.

Rex followed obediently, still not understanding where he was and exactly what was happening. A little farther inside the city, whose omni-colored lights were now veritably pulsating with energy, Morris began to explain, "When we heard you was comin', Frank and Kilmer come up with a plan to git you in, figurin' you probably wasn't carryin' any papers. That ol' boy at the gate can be a little tough on a man with no papers."

"Where am I?" asked Rex. "Is this heaven?"

"Well, no one calls it that, but I reckon it's prob'ly somethin' like that," answered Morris.

"Well, how'd Frank and Kilmer git in…and you, too?"

"Well, Kilmer got in 'cause he got religion later in life and remember that black feller Frank got into the knife fight with?"

"Yeah, Harm Slade."

"Well, it seems Harm found the Lord during that short time between when he got out of the hospital and when he died. He says if it wasn't for Frank, he'd a been sleepin' down there at the depot, or worse, for sure," said Morris.

"Ol' Harm's here," inquired Rex, "and he got Frank in?"

"That's about the size of it. Me, I walked up that road like you did and when the ol' boy at the gate asked me for my credentials, I didn't have any. He asked me for my name and I was scared if he saw who I was, I might not make it in. Remember when I worked for them Greenbergs 'fore we went into the plumbin' business, and ol' man Greenberg called me 'Maurice,' and the customers thought I was one of their family?"

"Yeah," Rex smiled, "I remember that. They sold plumbing supplies wholesale to the general public and most of the licensed plumbers in town wouldn't install their material and you worked out of the back of their warehouse and did installations for them."

"Yeah, that's right," said Morris. "Anyway, I told that feller at the gate I was 'Maurice Greenberg' and he started looking it up in his log and couldn't find it. Meanwhile, a group of folks had just come up the hill to the gate and he told me to stand aside while he checked their papers. After he was in the middle of checkin' them out, I saw he wasn't payin' attention to me and I just walked on in."

"Shit-fahr, Morris," cried Rex, "we're both up here with no documents?"

"Hell, Rex, I been up here for quite a spell and no one has said anything so far."

"Where's Effie? Did Leonard make it, too?"

"Do you remember that the old man used to say he was a 'hard-shell Baptist' and that he believed in 'once in grace, always in grace'?"

"Yeah, I remember that," said Rex. "I never knew exactly what that meant, though."

"It means that he believed that if he was ever once qualified to go to heaven, that no matter what he did after that, he still had a ticket in."

"Well, that don't sound right."

"Well, I reckon maybe it is," responded Morris. "They say he come up to the gate and they let 'im in, no questions asked."

"I'll be God damned."

"It's prob'ly best if you don't cuss much over here. Effie got in without even showing her papers, too. Did you know she never once said a cuss word or tasted a drop of liquor?"

"I reckon I did; she was a good ol' gal…salt of the earth…When can I go see her?"

"You can see her anytime you want. She stays up there in that palace up on that hill over yonder. Some of our sisters is up there and Leonard has the job of takin' care of whatever whim and fancy any of 'em might have."

"He didn't do much of that over there where we just come from," said Rex. "I reckon that's his payback."

"Reckon it prob'ly is," said Morris.

"Well, I want to go see Effie and git her to make me some biscuits and gravy," Rex replied. "I ain't had no biscuits and gravy since DeLois got sick."

"Shit, Rex, I hate to tell you this, but there ain't no biscuits and gravy here."

"What? No biscuits and gravy? Why wouldn't there be no biscuits and gravy?"

"'Cause everything here is made of light and energy. Nothin's solid, like over there on the other side, where we come from. If you want biscuits and gravy, you have to git in line and go back over there for it."

"So that's what them sleepy-eyed bastards was standin' in line for back there at the depot."

"Yeah, that's right…and it's a long line, too…some of 'em never even wake up and walk up here. The ones that do usually don't stay too long; they're usually itchin' to git back over to the other side, where there's sex and fame and such."

"Sex? There ain't no sex here?" said Rex.

"Naw. Hell, Rex, everybody here's just one sex. Sex is only on the other side."

"Well, shit-fahr, Morris…or should I say 'Maurice,' I gotta think about this. Sex is one thing, but God damn, man…no biscuits and gravy? That just about takes the cake."

"Yeah…there ain't no cake, neither."

"I pretty much figgered that out," replied Rex. "Hey, look at them dogs chasin' that hog," cried Rex. "Is that ol' Red and Curly?"

"Shore is," Morris said. "They all run like that most ever'day and then go curl up together in the tall grass over yonder and take a nap."

"So how long are we gonna be here?" asked Rex.

"Well, best as I kin tell, 'bout as long as we want to, 'til we git to thinkin' too much about biscuits and gravy and sex and drivin' Cadillacs and all them sorts of thangs we used to do. Then we have to go on back over there and do that 'til we git tard of that."

"Sounds like an endless circle. Is that all there is to life…and where's Jesus, anyway?"

"I ain't seen 'im," said Morris. "Some folks say he's in a higher place. Maybe that's the 'heaven' them preachers keep talkin' about…it's funny, but most of the preachers I know about are down there at the depot, waitin' for the train back to the other side."

"Well, I'm gonna stay here for a while and size things up," said Rex. "You ain't seen Miller, have you?"

"Naw, there ain't nothin' for Miller over here; he prob'ly caught the first train back, 'fore I even got here," Morris speculated.

"Well, all right then," Rex said as he began to feel at home in his new surroundings. "One thing though, Morris, 'fore you go. What do I do if they come-inse askin' me why I'm up here with no papers?"

"Do what we did when we come to California: don't tell 'em nothin'," Morris laughed as he slowly faded into the ether. "Don't tell 'em nothin'."

Epilogue

Rex wandered around his new surroundings for a time, enjoying his new-found freedom and lack of physical restrictions. This was indeed an interesting place, with many enjoyable pastimes and lights, colors and music far superior to anything he had ever seen or heard. He met many people he knew, not all from the recent life that he could remember.

One day he walked past a door with a sign that said, "Confused about the future? Come in and receive a free orientation." Rex, being curious, opened the door, walked in and was greeted by what seemed to him to be an angel. The angel seated Rex in the waiting room and, when his turn came, invited him to enter the orientation room. Seated behind a lighted altar sat a gentleman with shoulder length copper-colored hair, broad shouldered, trim at the waist, wearing only a loin cloth. The gentleman nodded to Rex to take the seat directly in front of him.

"I was expecting you, Mr. Tanner," said the gentleman.

"I didn't tell anyone I was coming. Why were you expecting me?

"That would take a long explanation. Why don't we get to why you're here first?"

"Well, I saw that sign on the door and I figgered maybe you can tell me where I am and how I got here and when I'll be leavin'."

"Why do you think you'll be leaving?"

"My brother Morris told me if I want biscuits and gravy, or sex, or a Cadillac, I'll have to leave here."

"Your brother Morris is correct."

"Say, what's your name?"

"You can call me Bob."

"So Bob, how's all this work? Why can't we have some biscuits and gravy while we're here?"

"Well, Rex, biscuits and gravy and all material things are products of and belong in the material world. This is the astral world; here everything is made of light and pranic energy. The material world is much grosser and considerably smaller in the grand scope of things."

"Well, I'll admit I like it here a lot, but then ag'in, I kind of miss some of the things I'm used to on the other side…the material world, as you call it."

"That's fine, Rex, you can go back whenever you please. You've been here a few hundred years by material world time; I can get you a ticket on the next train back right away."

"Wait a minute, Bob, I ain't sayin' I'm ready to go just yet. Several hundred years, --are you shittin' me?"

"Rex, you need to be more selective in your speech. Words, sounds, even thoughts, carry a vibration unique unto themselves and can cast a negative or positive energy on whatever you are using them to reference.

"Sorry about that, Bob, I reckon I do need to clean up my speech a bit. Effie was always gittin' on me about that back there in that material world."

"OK then, Rex, what could I tell you to help you get a clearer idea of what your purpose is in life?"

"Well, just tell me what the material world is."

"The material world is a manifestation, in a physical

realm, of the body of God."

"God has a body?"

"The entire physical creation is God's physical body."

"Where does it end?

"It doesn't end, Rex; it goes on forever."

"How can it?"

"It's God in the physical form. It has no beginning, end or limitations."

"So our material bodies are like God's?"

"That's an astute question, Rex. Yes, in fact, not only our physical bodies are patterned after God's, but our astral and causal bodies, too.

"Well, I reckon I'm out of my physical body and I can see I'm in my astral body, but 'causal' body? What's that?"

"That's the original body of ideas that God manifested when he created you."

"So, Bob, are you sayin' that God made me out of some ideas?"

"Yes, Rex, and when he merged them all together, he encased them in your astral body of energy and life force."

"And then he put that in my physical body?"

"Three bodies, that's right, Rex: one of subtle ideas, one of energy and one of gross physical matter."

"So if my astral body, which I'm in right now, dies, I'm still in my causal body?"

"You're beginning to understand, my son."

"Well, Bob, that's mighty interestin', but how do I git back to the material world?"

"That's easy, Rex, just focus on whatever physical desires you have and wait for a 'spark' that is appealing to you to occur and then jump into it."

"What happens then?"

"If you're successful, you become an embryo in the physical body of a woman in the material world."

"So if you want somethin' strong enough you can have it, then?"

"That's the nature of the physical world. It's not always immediate, though; sometimes it takes several lifetimes to attain your goals. In the meantime, you run the risk of creating more physical desires, which will continue to bind you to the material world."

"Several lifetimes--how many lifetimes do you have?"

"As many as it takes to work out your physical karma. It is said that it takes eight thousand earthly lifetimes in a human body to develop the capacity to ponder God."

"I reckon karma is what you got comin' for what you already done. I think I already figgered that one out. And then how many lifetimes to git back to Him?"

"Each soul is unique; some take longer than others. There are factors involved that can slow or accelerate your return."

"But what's the point of gittin' back, if you never run out of lifetimes?"

"God is irresistible. The closer you get to Him, the more love, joy and bliss you experience. It's a magnetic pull, infinitely stronger, more romantic and more intimate than any human attraction. It would not be correct to say that you are God, but it is true that God is you…and everyone else, too. All paths eventually return you to your Creator."

"I don't understand how time works. How long have there been people livin' on earth?"

"To begin with, Rex, time and space are illusions created by God to make you think you're separated from Him. In reality, God plays all the parts in His creation. It's only your ego, the 'you' that thinks it's separate from God and other human beings, that believes it's independent and alone. Earthly time occurs in 24,000 year cycles. Imagine a pie with slices of 12 degrees in width. At the bottom are two slices that represent the lowest point in human development. They straddle the midpoint of the bottom of the pie. This is called the "dark ages," or Kali Yuga. Man is confused and very ignorant during this period of time. Moving upward on both sides of the pie are double slices of 24 degrees which represent an "atomic age," or Dwapara Yuga. Those ages last for 2,400 years, and the intellect of man begins to awaken and explore its potential. Your last earthly sojourn ended 293 years into an ascending Dwapara Yuga. Humanity was just beginning to explore the dynamics and potentials of atomic energy. After the 2,400 year period is completed, a triple slice of 36 degrees, or 3,600 years, called a "magnetic age," or Treta Yuga, occurs on each side of the pie, where man advances beyond anything imaginable in the previous "lower ages." After that, the two remaining 48 degree slices of 4,800 years each, called Satya Yuga, occur as a spiritual, mental and physical "golden age," details of which you are not at this time capable of comprehending. The two 4,800 year "slices" straddle the center point of the top of the pie, one reaching its ultimate ascension and the other beginning the descent back through the lower ages."

"A twenty-four thousand year cycle--what happens after that?"

"The wheel, or pie as we're calling it here, continues to turn and the process continues over and over until humanity has liberated itself and this planet is no longer of any inhabitable use."

"How many times does it go around?"

"Up 'til now, Earth has gone through 83,000 of these 24,000 year cycles."

"That's almost two billion years! Are you serious?"

"Consider this, Rex: we've been talking about time, now let's consider space. At this time on the planet Earth, scientists are speculating that there are 800 billion stars in the Milky Way. The Earth's sun is one of the smaller stars.

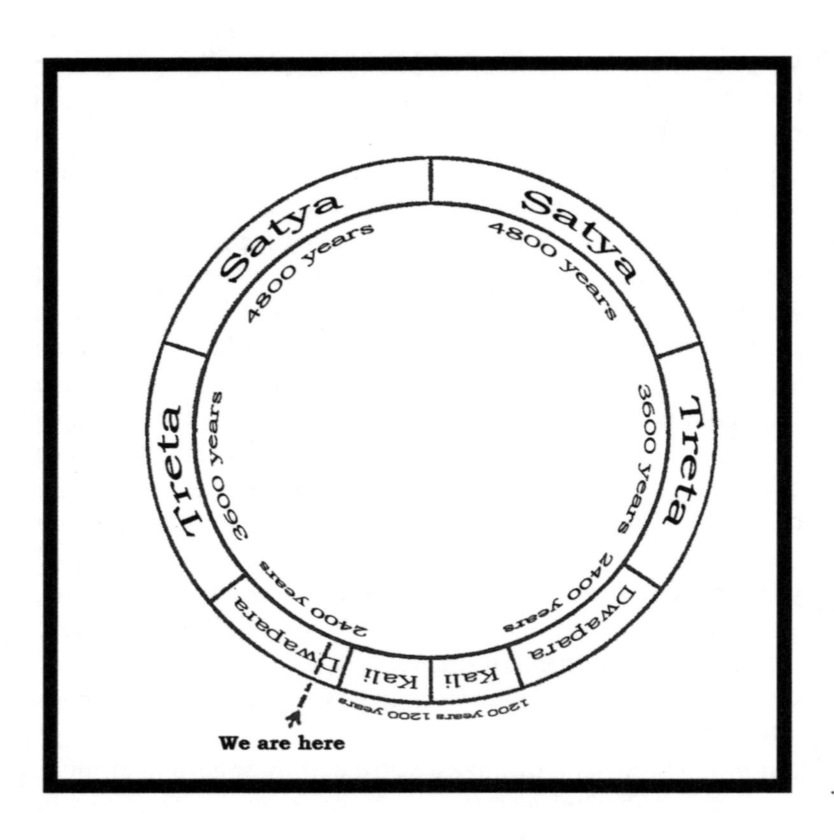
Satya
4800 years
Satya
4800 years
Treta
3600 years
Treta
3600 years
Dwapara
2400 years
Dwapara
2400 years
Kali
Kali
1200 years 1200 years
We are here

Beyond that, they calculate that there are 80 billion Milky Ways. The truth is that God continues to create and populate worlds of every shape, size and form. There is no real beginning or end to any of His endeavors. Since He is eternal and you are made in His image, you have no limitations, either. Getting back to our earlier conversation, the earth is only halfway through its projected lifespan."

"Another two billion years…that's a long time."

"It's only relative to the illusion God has created to entertain Himself through us; in reality, time and space don't exist."

"Well, Bob, you've given me a lot to think about. If I decide to go on back over to the other side, will I ever see you ag'in?"

"I'm on the other side too, Rex. It might be possible for you to find me. If not, I'll keep an eye out for you and help you try to stay out of trouble."

"I appreciate that, Bob, and all that you've told me, too. I reckon that was about the best 'orientation' I ever had."

With that, Rex instinctively bowed before the great Instructor, touched his feet and felt himself dissolve in a whirl of ecstatic reverie as he pondered an approaching, very attractive spark coming his way.

The Long Migration West

In the California green where I was born
Two thousand miles from the ragin' dust bowl storms
Proud and first born son
Of an outlaw Okie's blood
A generation from my grandpa's farm

In the California sun where I first grew
I learned the songs of the men as they passed through
And I came to love the best
Of that long migration west
They were lookin' for their place and I was too

You weather beaten brothers of the Oklahoma wind
Sit awhile and share your smile again
And all you lonesome heroes that stood up to the test
Your time has come to rest
While I sing your song of the long migration west

In the California valleys you can see
Orchards groves and vineyards endlessly
And the men who work the crops
Until the foggy winter drops
Ain't got a lot to do but wait 'til spring

And in the California cities you could die
Of loneliness just watchin' time pass by
And when it finally does
You just laugh out loud because
Nobody ever taught you how to cry

You weather beaten brothers of the Oklahoma wind
Sit awhile and share your smile again

And all you lonesome heroes that stood up to the test
Your time has come to rest
While I sing your song of the long migration west

In the California past as I look back
At the army tents and rows of one room shacks
Where my people got their start
Where my people gave their heart
While the California summers bent their backs

And in the California dirt where some now rest
Mute casualties of the long migration west
While their children carry on
While an old friend sings this song
While the California grass grows greener yet

Words & Music by Gary Rex Tanner

Songs from this book can be heard at
www.oklahomagamblinman.com

To hear songs written & performed by Gary Rex Tanner
Please visit www.garyrextanner.com

Many people don't really understand what an "Okie" is. Some think it's a person that lives, or was born, in Oklahoma, or sometimes they mean uneducated poor white folks. Specifically, an "Okie" is a person and a person's children who migrated from Oklahoma, Texas, Arkansas and sometimes Missouri to California between the years 1930 and 1950. With that definition in mind I dedicate this song to the following:

Charles Avery	Harold Avery	Howard Beleau
Bud Bishop	Carl Bishop	Logan Bishop
Louis Brink	Jim Catron	Elbert Gaines
Ray Gaines	Clarence Graham	Eldon Hawkins
Walter Heard	Connie Hightman	Joe Hopkins
Jim Horn	Earl Huffman	Elgin Huffman
Floyd Kelton	Curly Knight	Buster Knox
Leo Lane	Leon Lane	Jess McBroom
Bob McDaniel	Max McLemore	Dude Mowrey
George O'Rourke	Wendell Pennington	Les Phillips
George Postum	Mel Ratliff	Grover Rice
Henry Rice	Charles Riddle	Ed Ridenour
Jimmy Ridenour	J.W. Ritchie	John Sauls
Pete Sauls	Curly Seawright	Sylvester Shipman
Glen Stepp	Larry Taylor	Gordon Walk
Jerald Walk	Van Walk	Bruce Ward
Jimmy Ward	Ray Ward	Shorty Warthan
Wise Welch	Hamburger Bill	Punkin' Jim

About the Author

Gary & Daisy Tanner

Gary Rex is a second generation "Okie" born in Modesto, California before World War II who eschews the notion that the pursuit of celebrity enhances life's experiences in any positive aspect. He lives a somewhat reclusive life with his wife Daisy in a remote area of North San Diego County in California, overlooking a small lake with a majestic unobstructed view of Palomar Mountain.

Songs can be heard and Pictures & Paintings can be viewed at
www.oklahomagamblinman.com

To hear other songs written & performed by
Gary Rex Tanner
Please visit
www.garyrextanner.com

You can email us at: info@garyrextanner.com

Thank you!